Praise for *We're In This Together*

"Considering the need to close the gap between cost of delivery and certainty as to effectiveness of solution for the exceptional learner, Mark Claypool and John McLaughlin have taken on the oft-ignored but important support layer of private–public partnerships in the United States. There are no two more experienced curators of relevant and pragmatic information on this topic, which should be required reading for professionals and parents of up to 20 percent of the national student population." —**Frank A. Bonsal**, director of entrepreneurship, Towson University

"As both a business owner and advocate for the advancement of Chicago's youth, I have seen the impact private business partnerships can make on a community level firsthand. In large and diverse urban markets, a multifaceted approach to education is absolutely necessary to meet the needs of our young people. *We're In This Together* provides a fresh perspective on the ways non-traditional partnerships can provide solutions to address complex issues within our educational systems." —**Derrick Taylor**, president of the Black McDonald's Operators Association of Chicagoland and Northwest Indiana

"The higher the standards, the greater the gap, the more public-private partnerships are needed to reach America's academic goals and fulfill every student's dream for the future! Meet two of this nation's greatest visionaries, Mark Claypool and John McLaughlin, who are determined to accomplish both for every learner in every classroom throughout the United States. These two tenacious education leaders have authored a most timely book that educators, parents, advocates, Congress and every education stakeholder must read. They insightfully and sensitively define the past, shed light on the present and illuminate a path for every student who is challenged to attain a quality education in our public schools. I hope we all listen, hear, and act on their clarion call for all of our children." —**Kathleen Leos**, president/CEO, the Global Institute for Language and Literacy Development, LLC

"This book covers in detail a virtually unexplored 'third rail' of special education services for school districts. Through interviews with stakeholders on 'both sides' that have successfully collaborated and improved options and services for students, families and school employees, this book delivers a new and fresh view that will be of value to the overwhelming majority of our nation's 14,000-plus school districts that have not explored these opportunities." —**Bruce H. Miles**, EdD, Big River Group, LLC

"Congrats to John McLaughlin and Mark Claypool for this groundbreaking book that shares the many challenges public schools face today and explores how private, often for-profit companies can provide the help needed to ensure more at-risk students can indeed find success." —**Peter Ruppert**, CEO, Fusion Education Group

WE'RE IN THIS TOGETHER

Public–Private Partnerships in Special and At-Risk Education

Mark K. Claypool and John M. McLaughlin

ROWMAN & LITTLEFIELD
Lanham • Boulder • New York • London

Published by Rowman & Littlefield
A wholly owned subsidiary of The Rowman & Littlefield Publishing Group,
Inc.
4501 Forbes Boulevard, Suite 200, Lanham, Maryland 20706
www.rowman.com

Unit A, Whitacre Mews, 26-34 Stannary Street, London SE11 4AB

British Library Cataloguing in Publication Information Available

Library of Congress Cataloging-in-Publication Data

Claypool, Mark.
We're in this together : public-private partnerships in special and at-risk-education / Mark K.
Claypool and John M. McLaughlin.
pages cm.
Includes bibliographical references.
ISBN 978-1-4758-1447-7 (cloth : alk. paper) — ISBN 978-1-4758-1448-4 (pbk. : alk. paper) —
ISBN 978-1-4758-1449-1 (electronic) 1. Children with disabilities—Education—United States. 2.
Public schools—United States. 3. Public-private sector cooperation—United States. I. McLaugh-
lin, John M. II. Title.
LC4031.C595 2015
371.9—dc23

2015009668

♾ ™ The paper used in this publication meets the minimum requirements of
American National Standard for Information Sciences Permanence of Paper
for Printed Library Materials, ANSI/NISO Z39.48-1992.

Printed in the United States of America

CONTENTS

FOREWORD

Barbara Byrd-Bennett

It has been my privilege to dedicate more than 40 years to a career in public education as a teacher, principal, district executive officer, and superintendent in four school systems, and with boards or organizations commissioned to improve educational outcomes for public-school students. Authors Mark Claypool and John McLaughlin are genuine innovators who illustrate how partnering with private companies that share our goal to improve student outcomes, especially for the most vulnerable learners, can be instrumental to student success.

Their book, *We're in This Together: Public–Private Partnerships in Special and At-Risk Education* is vital to understanding how relationships between school districts and private companies can benefit students, school districts, and students' families and communities.

I was raised in a working-class family and attended New York City public schools. I graduated from high school prepared for college and inspired to teach. After several years of teaching, I became a school principal and in that position, became more aware of the political, personal, and administrative aspects of school leadership. While education has changed during the last 30 years, three truths are as relevant today as when I entered my first classroom as a young teacher.

Truth #1: The work is hard. I became a teacher because I was passionate about student learning. I learned early the importance of engaging all stakeholders, including those in the private sector, to make the work "less hard" for teachers and administrators, and more beneficial for students and families. Some of the hardest work for public-school teachers and administrators involves creating programming for students whose achievement is most at risk, such as students with disabilities and students who need options for earning a high-school diploma.

Truth #2: "Doing more with less" is just the way it is in the public sector. I spent nearly my entire career in public-school systems where most of the students could be considered at risk due to poverty, violence, drugs, inadequate health care, unemployment, and breakdowns in family systems. No matter where I was and no matter how complex the environment, I was always charged to "do more with less."

When I became CEO of Chicago Public Schools in April 2012, CPS had a billion-dollar deficit. I could not cut my way out of it or ask my staff to do more with less, but I could explore partnerships to help get the system right-side up and provide effective programs for students. After reading this book, I better understand that public–private partnerships are neither good nor bad. They are tools that offer accountability, flexibility, an expanded scope of services, responsible stewardship of finite resources, and improved outcomes for students and families. Our vision in CPS is that every student in every neighborhood will be engaged in a rigorous, well-rounded instructional program and will graduate prepared for success in college, career, and life. This vision cannot be realized in the district's current operational state without the support of private-sector partners.

Truth #3: Making education work for ALL children is the most important political, societal, economic, and social justice issue of the twenty-first century. It is clear that Mark and John believe this too, and they show us how to build productive partnerships to address these issues.

I have worked in some of the largest and most challenged school systems in the country, and without question, some of our successes in those districts are due to strong strategic partnerships. If school systems in Chicago, New York, Detroit, and Cleveland can benefit from these relationships, then all systems can.

I encourage district leaders throughout the country to overcome what they perceive as obstacles to public–private partnerships and see with fresh eyes that private organizations work in cooperation with us, not in competition, in order to help decrease dropout rates, increase graduation rates, and provide services to students with special needs.

Mark and John have devoted their careers to education innovation, and they have written an outstanding playbook for all of us in public education.

December 2014

PREFACE/AUTHORS' NOTE

This book is designed as qualitative research in line with the tradition of ethnographic participant observation. Both authors are involved on a daily basis in public–private partnerships in the study area of special and at-risk education. The methodology involved identifying and interviewing four dozen professionals knowledgeable about public–private partnerships. These professionals ranged from public-school district administrators to state superintendents, from private company heads to professional association leaders, and from attorneys to professors. One of the interviews was conducted in person and the remainder of the interviews were conducted by phone. The interviews were conducted between June and December 2014.

ACRONYMS

AASA	American Association of School Administrators
ABA	Applied Behavior Analysis
ACES	Austin Centers for Exceptional Students
APBA	Association of Professional Behavior Analysts
ARD	Admission, Review, and Dismissal
ASBO	Association of School Business Officials International
ASHA	American Speech-Language-Hearing Association
BACB	Behavior Analyst Certification Board
BCaBA	Board Certified Assistant Behavior Analyst
BCBA	Board Certified Behavior Analyst
BOCES	Boards of Cooperative Educational Services
CAPSES	California Association of Private Special Education Schools
CASA	Council of Affiliated State Association
CCC	Certificate of Clinical Competence in Speech-Language Pathology
CFR	Code of Federal Regulations
CIS	Communities In Schools
CPS	Chicago Public Schools

DCPS	District of Columbia Public Schools
EAP	Early Autism Project
ED	Emotional Disturbance
EIA	Education Industry Association
ERDI	Education Research and Development Institute
ESA	Educational Services of America
ESL	English as a Second Language
FAPE	Free Appropriate Public Education
GAAP	Generally Accepted Accounting Principles
GNETS	Georgia Network for Education and Therapeutic Supports
IAEP	Interim Alternative Education Placement
IDEA	Individuals with Disabilities Education Act
IEP	Individualized Education Program
LAUSD	Los Angeles Unified School District
LCI	Licensed Children's Institution
LEA	Local Educational Agency
LRE	Least-Restrictive Environment
MAAPS	Massachusetts Association of 766 Approved Private Schools
NAPSEC	National Association of Private Special Education Centers
NCCA	National Commission for Certifying Agencies
NCES	National Center for Education Statistics
NCLB	No Child Left Behind
NCPPP	National Council for Public-Private Partnerships
NISD	Northside Independent School District
NPDC	National Professional Development Center
NPS	Non-Public Schools
NSBA	National School Boards Association
OIG	Office of Inspector General

OSEP	Office of Special Education Programs
PPP	Public-private Partnership
RBT	Registered Behavior Technician
RFP	Requests for Proposal
SBO	School Business Officer
SCEAP	South Carolina Early Autism Project
SELPA	Special Education Local Plan Area
SES	Supplemental Education Services
SESI	Specialized Educational Services, Inc.
SLP	Speech-Language Pathologist
SPED	Special Education Director
SPG	Speech Pathology Group
SPLC	Southern Poverty Law Center
STEM	Science, Technology, Engineering, and Math
TEACCH	Treatment and Education of Autistic and Related Communication Handicapped Children
UCP	United Cerebral Palsy
USDOE	United States Department of Education

1

TODAY'S PUBLIC SCHOOLS

Doing More with Less

You can observe a lot just by watching. —*Yogi Berra*

Every public-school principal, district superintendent, and school board member today has spent his or her entire administrative service muddling through the constantly changing demands and expectations of the Education Reform Era. For years, reforms focused on increased expectations with increased fiscal support underwriting the anticipated improvements. Now the mantra is "do more with less"—a theme that seems likely to persist given the economic, demographic, and political aspects of America in this second decade of the twenty-first century.

Today's educators face mounting performance expectations with fiscal constraints, constantly changing technologies that reshape the classroom and the school, vigorous debate about national standards, and an increasing flow of non-English-language speakers into the classrooms. It's familiar ground for America's public schools. Controversy, new purposes, and expanding responsibilities have been the norm since public education was established.

The development of public education has been a glorious achievement, but at every step in its progress, every turn in the road, there has been substantial and often vitriolic bickering. From the first mandates of compulsory elementary education to the expansion to high schools, from the inclusion to the exclusion of religion, from states' rights to the federal role, from local property taxes to equity funding, from the inclusion of the differently abled to desegregation to sex education to afterschool programs and on and on, the evolution of public education has garnered passionate attention at the local, state, and national levels.

Even by historical standards, America's attention to public education during the past 30 years has been intense and sustained. Taking the 1983 release of *A Nation at Risk* as the beginning of the Education Reform Era, the collective effort to improve schools and to increase reading levels, graduation rates, and science literacy is unprecedented. If the period of the 1950s through the 1970s was devoted to access and equity, the period since 1983 has been focused on attempting to make good on the promise of excellence in public education.

While the voices in the Education Reform Era have been as varied as the nation's population, for simplicity's sake, two broad camps have stood out in the cacophony: those focused on raising reading levels and elevating students and society with improved public schools, and those demanding higher accountability for school performance and a clearer return on investment for taxpayers. Also emblematic of this era has been the rise of the federal role in setting expectations, if not standards, in an array of administrative, organizational, and curricular matters, despite contributing only 8 percent of the funding for America's public schools.

Today's school leaders find themselves in the same position as their predecessors: dancing to music set for them by forces far beyond their control. That is not a statement of hopelessness or self-pity. It is a statement of what is. However, today's school leaders also have tools that were not available to their predecessors. Among those tools are fingertip access to research and best practices, lightning-speed communications, and the best-educated teacher force in the nation's history. Furthermore, today's educational administrators have a tool of leadership—rallying the underdog—that addresses the tenor of the nation and a public education system under attack.

Pam Homan, the superintendent of the Sioux Falls, South Dakota, public schools, notes that one of her top jobs is to support the district's teachers by cutting through the noise of anger and hostility directed toward public schools, dispel the accusation that public schools are failing, and let the teachers know they are doing a good job and have much to be proud of and many accomplishments to their credit. Put succinctly, Homan said, "The national agenda says public schools have failed. My role is to tell them (district teachers) that they haven't failed" (personal communication, June 16, 2014).

How does Homan do this? She uses resources in her community and across the nation that allow her teachers and staff to focus on the students. She is a believer in public–private partnerships. Her district of 22,000 students recently entered a cutting-edge partnership with Avera Health Systems to increase the quality and expand students' access to health care. Sensitive to the possible misgivings of the district's school nurses, Homan helped them understand that the partnership with Avera improves the district by enhancing services, saving money, and increasing the effective reach of each nurse.

"It's all about territory," she noted. Homan put a program on steady ground that could have been seen as a claim jump. For her, cooperation with private companies makes sense. "In the complexity of society today, partnering with private companies is a win-win because the public schools can't be taxed any further."

Public–private partnerships are used widely outside the classroom, but with public schooling at its limits and no relief in sight regarding the expansion of responsibilities, education leaders must consider every possible means to address the demands of the day. How schools and school districts can leverage the power of such partnerships is the focus of this book. But first, a few words about partnerships.

THE BASICS OF PUBLIC–PRIVATE PARTNERSHIPS

The word *partnership* engenders warm and positive feelings. Batman and Robin, Sears and Roebuck, Bert and Ernie, Butch and Sundance, Jobs and Wozniak, Ben and Jerry, Franklin and Eleanor, Ferdinand and Isabella. Some partnerships are so ingrained in American culture that one name can hardly be said without the other: Hope and Crosby, Rodgers and Hammerstein, Simon and Garfunkel, Lewis and Clark. Successful partnerships are wonderful.

But within the collective memory of great partnerships, none involve a partnership between a private company and a public-school district. While thousands of such public–private partnerships (PPPs) exist, they do not rise to a level of fame or familiarity.

This book focuses on PPPs that have the potential to make a real difference in an important part of our society: the education of struggling students, including students with handicapping conditions, students with autism, and students at risk of school failure. We cover a wide array of partnerships, drawing on occasion from the experiences of Educational Services of America (ESA), a company with more than 40 years of experience partnering with school districts. We also offer a glimpse of what could be the future of such partnerships in a rapidly evolving public education arena.

In moving forward, defining public–private partnerships is crucial but simple. A broader discussion of PPPs is offered in chapter 2, but for now the following description of PPPs will suffice: *public–private partnerships are contractual arrangements between governmental agencies and private companies for the execution of specific projects or services.*

PPPs have been established in many aspects and levels of government for decades. From the management of mundane matters such as garbage hauling, grounds maintenance, snow removal, and parking meter operation, to more complex functions like running waste treatment facilities, processing crime reports, and delivering social services, local governments participate in a variety of PPPs. The National Council for Public–Private Partnerships noted that, "The average American city works with private partners to perform 23 out of 65 basic municipal services" (NCPPP 2014).

State and federal governments embrace PPPs for matters as widespread as nation-building responsibilities in developing countries and infrastructure development to more specific matters like airport security screenings. Federal agencies like the Environmental Protection Agency, the Transportation Security Administration, the Department of Defense, and the Veterans Administration, and organizations like the U.S. Conference of Mayors all engage in PPPs.

PPPs are neither good nor bad; they are tools government organizations such as public-school districts can choose to use. To be successful, they should be cost-effective for the organization and provide a quality of production, development, or service at least equal to that provided by a fully government-run service. They require diligence on the part of the government agencies from the beginning of the possibility of entering a PPP and throughout its execution. PPPs are not panaceas but are contractual agreements and as such are only as good as the entities between which they are created.

Public-school districts already use PPPs extensively for student transportation, food service, and custodial services; Students First, Aramark, and ServiceMaster are familiar names in many school districts across the country. But school districts partner with small, owner-operated enterprises or midsize businesses as often as they contract with the national corporations, and they engage in PPPs far beyond the areas of transportation, food, and cleaning services. School districts enter PPPs every time they need something that cannot be produced with district personnel, including legal services, health services, building and grounds maintenance, environmental management, facilities construction, risk and insurance management, after-school care, telecommunications, and many other functions.

An area that does not readily come to mind when considering PPPs within public education is instruction. The instruction of students is almost universally conducted by school district employees, yet special education is a qualified exception and, to a lesser degree, so is the education of students at risk.

This book focuses on PPPs that address students with special-education needs, students who are at risk, and students with autism. The three most significant reasons schools enter into a PPP for these services are the same reasons that drive the decision for most areas covered under a PPP: expertise, accountability, and cost management. But there are many reasons beyond these three that encourage a district to consider a PPP for special education or for the education of at-risk students. Done correctly, PPPs expand the options and control for a school district.

Among the benefits of PPPs:

- Increased control—PPPs are contractual arrangements in which the school district holds the balance of power. As such, the district has the opportunity to create the service or solution it seeks. It is a clean-slate agreement.
- Enhanced accountability—PPPs are designed to accomplish objectives that the district has not done successfully or has not been able to attempt. A PPP should include clear measures of perfor-

mance accountability and how and when those measures will be taken.

- Good stewardship of resources—PPPs should be cost-effective. Public schools use fund accounting, which focuses on accountability. Private enterprise uses GAAP (generally accepted accounting principles), which focuses on profitability. Fund accounting does not lend itself to measuring cost-effectiveness. Nonetheless, administrators must see the creation of a PPP as a good and effective use of public resources.
- Leveraged market capacities—As varied as school districts are, few are robust incubators of fresh ideas or promoters of out-of-the-box thinking. The United States is among the richest nations in the world when it comes to market-driven solutions. This can be to the advantage of school districts.
- Increased flexibility—Using PPPs gives a school district a wider menu from which to choose. It also allows a district to make shorter-term commitments of one to five years.
- Expanded scope of services—If a district is not sure a service is needed or how it might be shaped or staffed, a PPP is a good way to test the water. Perhaps the private partner stays indefinitely with the district or perhaps the district takes over the service under a scheduled working arrangement.
- Extended local control—A PPP is an extension of local control, not an abdication. School districts too frequently believe that asking an outside firm to help it address a specific academic issue is an admission of failure rather than a demonstration of the commitment to meeting the needs of its students.
- Increased competitiveness—Entering a PPP for a specific academic service makes a district more market-competitive. A PPP provides options to the traditional school format and options for students and families.

PPPs for children with exceptionalities have been part of the landscape for nearly two centuries. As public education developed in the mid-nineteenth century, so did advocacy groups for the deaf, blind, and mentally impaired. These groups established schools and residential programs that provided services for the differently abled fortunate enough to live near such programs or to secure access to them. These nonpublic operations provided education, training, and life-skill programming that did not become mandatory for public schools until 1975, when President Gerald Ford signed PL 94-142, the Education for All Handicapped Children Act.

The intersection of public and private, the synergy between public and private, the cooperation between, the balance between, the relationship between public and private evolves with the times, sensitivities, court clarifications, and economic pressures. ESA is perhaps the nation's most experienced organization in creating and executing partnerships that involve classroom instruction for at-risk and special-education students. ESA operates approximately 200 schools and programs in partnership with school districts in 25 states.

But by no means is ESA alone in the provision of such services in partnership with public-school districts. Other companies that participate in PPPs with school districts include arc, a provider of after-school learning, experiential, and development opportunities for school districts in California; Specialized Educational Services, Inc., which operates 55 schools and programs for special education and alternative education populations in 11 states and Washington, D.C.; Camelot, which provides alternative and special-education programming for middle and secondary students in partnerships with districts across the country; Communities In Schools, a national nonprofit that partners with about 190 schools and communities in 26 states devoted to helping at-risk students graduate; and ACES, a provider of special-education services for public-school students with a variety of handicapping conditions from 23 school districts in the Phoenix region. These and other companies are profiled in chapter 3.

PRIVATIZATION: THAT FOUR-LETTER WORD

A PPP can be viewed as a contract, as a measured choice for a government entity, or as privatization. Few words are as loaded in public education as privatization. Blood pressures rise, tempers flare, and political colors fly when the "P" word makes an appearance.

For more than three decades, the idea of privatizing government services has drifted in and out of public debate and has ebbed into dozens of functions traditionally seen as government services. Twenty years ago, Thomas Shannon (1995), the executive director of the National School Boards Association, sounded the alarm at the opening of the 1995–1996 school year, linking privatization with the rise of charter and for-profit schools.

The concept of privatization not only carries emotional baggage, it is an amorphous, poorly defined, and often misused word. Joseph Murphy, cited by *Education Week* in 2014 as a Top Ten Edu-Scholar, has addressed a variety of critical and often understudied aspects of American schooling in his work. In *The Privatization of Schooling: Problems and Possibilities* (Murphy 1996) he provides a sound framework for addressing the historical context, underpinnings, and definition of privatization. While Murphy offers dozens of definitions of privatization from leading scholars, one seems to fit this book best for its simplicity and conversational tone—a definition that Stuart Butler (1992, 24), writing in William Gormley's *Privatization and Its Alternatives*, offered: *"In fact, all we are really talking about with privatization is making the private sector available, in some form, for achieving public objectives."*

ADDRESSING THE OBVIOUS HEAD-ON

Putting pen to paper is an act of consolidating thoughts, making a case, expressing a point of view. In today's polarized political environment, black-and-white positions prevail. Black folding into white or white into black hardly exists. The case made in this book is for public-education leaders to embrace education-company expertise for the benefit of students. The articles cited and the sources quoted generally, but not exclusively, support that viewpoint. Some may disagree with the message and cite other sources that support their disagreement. That is the nature of discourse.

A variety of opinions exist on the topic of PPPs. This has been the case with each measure that has expanded the responsibilities of public schools or enhanced the tools educators have had to provide the finest opportunities for their students. This book is penned by two authors who are on the private-company side of the public–private equation. We believe that dropout rates are higher, graduation rates are lower, special-education services are more limited, and students' lives are wasted because of the many obstacles and prejudices that work against PPPs that involve interfacing with students in the classroom.

Thus, while the impact this book has on the environment of public education will be impossible to measure, its message is offered in the spirit of open dialogue with the belief that the education of some of America's most vulnerable students is everyone's business. This book is written because lower dropout rates for at-risk students and better services for students with multiple handicaps are in our nation's best interest regardless of the delivery mechanism. All good educators want what is best for students. The quality of life for millions of students and the attendant benefits to society hang in the balance.

SHALL WE MOVE ON?

This book is designed to support school leaders who are asked to do more with less. Chapter 2 addresses the complexity of determining what is public and what is private in today's world of public schooling and surveys the gamut of emotions and organizational allegiances that color the environment for PPPs focused on instruction.

Chapter 3 offers profiles of a variety of companies that partner with school districts in the service of children with special needs and students at risk of school failure. For-profits and nonprofits as well as national and regional firms are presented.

Contracts for the private delivery of special education services are the focus of chapter 4. While almost a matter of routine in some states, the use of private special schools to meet FAPE (free appropriate public education) and LRE (least-restrictive environment) requirements is infrequent in other states and for reasons that go beyond population density and the availability of private providers.

While chapter 4 addresses special education, the rise of the number of children with autism, the development of legislation in three-fourths of the states mandating insurance coverage for behavioral treatment, and the evolution of the discipline of behavior analysis calls for a chapter focused solely on this complex issue. Autism is the focus of chapter 5.

Chapter 6 explores PPPs that address the educational needs of students at risk. The term "at risk" is defined and the staggering number of students who fall into that category is addressed. A review of public-school programs for at-risk students, national studies, and sample PPP programs shows the breadth and depth of this large and expanding slice of education.

The concluding chapter 7 wraps up what has been offered and presents an idea for what might evolve from the recent past. A vision is offered for an era when sense is restored to public education, when confidence is raised, when performance is enhanced, when lines between public education and private enterprise become irrelevant, when mass-produced education becomes mass customized, and when the focus of the mission evolves from public education to the education of the public.

REFERENCES

Butler, S. 1991. Privatization for public purposes. In *Privatization and Its Alternatives*, ed. William Gormley Jr. Madison: University of Wisconsin Press.

Murphy, J. 1996. *The Privatization of Schooling*. Thousand Oaks, CA: Sage Publications.

National Council of Public–Private Partnerships. 2014. Top Ten Facts About PPPs. Retrieved at http://www.ncppp.org/ppp-basics/top-ten-facts-about-ppps/.

Shannon, T. 1995. Privatization presents a challenge to public schools. *School Board Notes* (2) 6.

2

PUBLIC–PRIVATE PARTNERSHIPS
America's Favorite Complicated Relationship

*To have done no man a wrong . . . to walk and live, unseduced,
within arm's length of what is not your own, with nothing between
your desire and its gratification but the invisible law of rectitude—
this is to be a man. —Orison Swett Marden*

Public education has a Gordian knot relationship with the private sector. Separating what is public and what is private is a matter of semantics, perspectives, and prejudices. Taxes are private monies gathered for the public good. School construction is underwritten by a bonding process that gives private investors the opportunity to profit from the construction, expansion, or renovation of public-school facilities. Many of the textbook companies that provide the basic tools of learning are publicly traded, dividend-yielding publishing conglomerates. Six of the seven largest publishing companies are based in Europe, among them, Pearson, Reed Elsevier, and Random House. The largest U.S.-based publishing company, by revenue, is eighth-ranked McGraw-Hill (*Publishers Weekly* 2013).

U.S. public schools spend between $7 billion and $8 billion per year on textbooks. London-based Pearson PLC is the largest provider of those texts. Pearson's CEO, John Fallon, made just under $3 million in 2013, according to *BusinessWeek*'s Executive Profile. Ron Packard, founder and former CEO of K12, Inc., averaged about $2 million annually. Packard's earnings were a frequent target of anger from those who saw him as profiting from public education. John Fallon's salary never makes the news, even though the price of textbooks has risen 800 percent in the past 30 years, according to the Bureau of Labor Statistics (cited in Band 2013). While Pearson PLC is a gigantic company compared to K12, Inc., just who gets picked on for being a public-school robber baron is interesting.

The materials of schooling, the supplies within the building, the office machines, lab equipment, laptops, desktops, football helmets, floor wax, lightbulbs, toilet paper, and #2 pencils were all procured from for-profit companies. In many school districts, private companies manage the payroll, manage the substitute teachers, and manage the facilities and the teacher retirement funds. Separating public and private interests in public education, deciding who are the good guys and who are the bad guys, is indeed a Gordian knot.

Within the complicated relationship between public education and private enterprise, bright red lines have been drawn on the ethics, morality, or appropriateness of private sector involvement in the delivery of public education. Shapiro (2013, 95) noted, "Also, a prevailing concern, to put it badly, is that private organizations will try to grab profit off our tax dollars, which to some extent has occurred."

Tienken and Orlich (2013, 42) place adoption of business values among the frauds being played upon American public education:

> We boldly suggest that business values are not appropriate to drive American education. True, we all want the most efficient use of the tax-payer dollar in the public schools. But that is not an education core value. Certainly, parents want their children to receive that elusive "best of educations." But business-like competitive practices are unlikely to provide it. Democracy is not efficient and thus, a democratic education is not efficient. In fact it is the inefficiency in the system that perhaps produces some of its greatest qualities among American students: creativity and innovation.

Rose (2014, 76) expressed skepticism of business being too involved in schooling:

> Some businesses have a direct financial incentive in matters educational. No question, the result has been some very good instructional materials and technological tools, but the moment commerce enters

the picture, there is the danger of the profit motive trumping educational goals.

Indeed, skepticism of market measures gaining strength in public education is strong and can be volatile. Charter schools, virtual schools, and vouchers are some of the most incendiary issues of the past 20 years. Research has been wide and deep on these three flammable topics and can be used to support a position from yea to nay and anywhere in between. An ailment of our time is that research is too often the pawn of policy.

But PPPs focused on special education and at-risk students are not examples of market forces unleashed, unchecked, or run amok. Indeed, such PPPs should strengthen the hand of the public-school district. Unlike charters, vouchers, or virtual schools, the locus of control remains with the public school board.

WHO'S GOOD AND WHO'S BAD? CHECK WITH YOUR ORGANIZATION

The National School Boards Association (NSBA), which represents more than 90,000 local school board members from 13,500 school districts, offers guidance on creating partnerships with private providers. As part of its series on School Board Governance, the NSBA published *Guidelines for Contracting with Private Providers for Educational Services* (1995) written by a coauthor of this book, J. M. McLaughlin. The booklet explores reasons a school district might consider contracted services, factors to be taken into account, and criteria to drive a decision. "This booklet is designed to assist school boards and superintendents in understanding issues related to contracting for administrative and teaching services and to offer guidance in how relationships might be formed with private companies" (NSBA 1995, 2).

About one-half of the nation's school superintendents are members of the American Association of School Administrators (AASA), which copublished the booklet noted above. However, on the home page of AASA's website from at least May to October 2014, AASA Executive Director Dan Domenech posted on the "Director's Corner":

The Superintendent is the voice for all the children in the community, including the many children who would have no voice if not for the Superintendent. Today, more than ever, America's Superintendents have the awesome responsibility to protect public education from the private and political interests that regard our schools as investment opportunities for corporate gains rather than fostering the American tradition of an educated community that is the core of our democratic process. (Domenech 2014)

While the AASA has its guard up for those interested in profiting from public education, Domenech's statement is not aimed at PPPs. "That statement has to do with the past 6 to 12 years of organizing initiatives and companies who were after public dollars. There was a huge infusion of public dollars into education," Domenech said, referring to Supplemental Educational Services (SES) that came on the scene in the No Child Left Behind (NCLB) package. Initially the SES dollars were restricted to private providers both for-profit and nonprofit. Domenech is also aggressive toward non-district-authorized charter schools, especially "online schools and fly-by-night programs that have left kids stranded" as they closed or failed to keep standard academic records to follow students to their next schools. But when it comes to PPPs for special-education students and students at risk of dropping out, he is not on the attack.

"We as an organization acknowledge that schools can't do it alone. Public–private partnerships in education are necessary and are an asset to serve the needs of the community," Domenech stated. "But in dealing with 50 states, I know there is huge variation in education models and in using PPPs."

Before assuming the leadership of AASA, Domenech served as a superintendent for more than 27 years, first on Long Island, then for a Board of Cooperative Educational Services (BOCES), a New York intermediary unit, and most recently as a superintendent in Fairfax County, Virginia. "Fairfax has outstanding special education programs and facilities yet I am familiar with meeting the needs of an IEP beyond the district. And Fairfax had a $2.4 billion budget; small districts are at a loss. There are still some districts in this country that are third world. There are huge discrepancies in how schools serve students with special needs. The quality of the programs has a lot to do with the zip code.

Massachusetts has standards and Mississippi has standards, but never the two shall meet" (personal communication, September 9, 2014).

Indeed, as Domenech noted, America has rich schools and poor schools. As the $630 billion public-education sector rolls along, millions of people rely on it for their livelihood and hundreds of thousands of companies do the same. And within both public schools and private companies there are bad actors. Rich districts, poor districts, charter schools, or private enterprise, it doesn't matter, money can trump both reason and a love of schooling. Free enterprise has no monopoly on greed and public education no monopoly on virtue. A cursory Internet search of the 2013–2014 school year revealed charges of embezzlement by public-school administrators in Rialto, Stockton, and San Francisco, California; Fairfax County, Virginia; Readsboro, Vermont; Chicago, Illinois; Beaumont, Texas; and Hartsdale and New York City, New York.

A cafeteria worker in Fulton County, Georgia, was charged with stealing more than $1 million during a 15-year period. The superintendent of Wall Schools in Freehold, New Jersey, was indicted on fraud, theft, and official misconduct. An elementary-school principal in Oklahoma City, Oklahoma, was charged with Medicaid fraud. The former head of the local teachers' association in Wight County, Virginia, was charged with embezzlement.

A Seattle (Washington) Public Schools official pleaded guilty to 36 counts of theft. A principal of a celebrated Baltimore high school was convicted of stealing $2 million, intended for disadvantaged children, in his previous job with Georgia's Department of Early Care and Learning. A Detroit Public Schools teacher and accountant were found guilty of money laundering and fraud.

Operators of a charter school in Washington, D.C., were accused of self-dealing and directing $3 million in charter funds to other closely tied companies. The FBI raided 19 charter schools in Ohio managed by a single company on a "white collar crime" investigation. In October 2013, the USDOE Office of Inspector General, Investigation Services, issued its Final Management Information Report on Fraud in Title I-Funded Tutoring Programs. The report stated:

> Over the past 5 years, the Office of Inspector General (OIG) has responded to a significant increase in cases of fraud and corruption among SES providers. In 2009, we had only one SES investigation: since then, we have received complaints for another 31 matters for

investigation, and this trend is continuing. These investigations are complex and resource-intensive, and they often involve large dollar losses. Additionally, they involve a significant public trust issue: our investigations have found many instances of public school teachers who have engaged in fraudulent conduct while working for SES providers.

This report focuses on our investigation work, which has found falsification of billing and attendance records, corruption by public officials, conflicts of interest related to recruiting students, conflicts of interest related to public school officials who are employed by an SES provider in non-instructional positions, and the use of improper financial incentives to enroll students. (USDOE 2013, 4)

Accusations of systematic cheating on high-stakes tests are under examination in the New York, Atlanta, Las Vegas, Philadelphia, and Washington, D.C., public schools. There is an investigation of data-rigging in a half dozen school districts in Ohio. Clearly, greed and malfeasance know no boundaries between the for-profit and public sectors. Nonetheless, a bias against for-profit companies exists.

Indeed, Superintendent Pam Homan of Sioux Falls says that mistrust "is what we have to break down and dismantle" (personal communication, June 16, 2014). Hostility to the private companies that can assist in meeting the needs of schools and students insults the foundation upon which public education rests: public taxes. Hostility to for-profit company involvement with public education tells American enterprise to keep paying the taxes but stay out of the business of education. That function belongs to the incumbents.

The Education Research and Development Institute (ERDI) perceives the interface of public education and private providers as critical to building a better system of education. The stated purpose of ERDI reads: "Our mission is to provide a forum for dialogue between outstanding educational leaders and committed corporate partners to shape products, goods, and services that will inspire excellence in education and enrich the achievement of all learners" (Education Research and Development Institute 2014).

Paul Dulle is ERDI's president and CEO. He came to the role after serving as an assistant superintendent in St. Louis County, Missouri, and as executive director of the Southwest Cooperative for Special Education in Chicago's southwestern suburbs. He also served as president and CEO of United Cerebral Palsy (UCP) of Greater Chicago and is now CEO of the UCP Seguin Foundation of Greater Chicago. In all those roles, he led innovative collaborative efforts to create new initiatives with no money and to create new wealth for districts and nonprofits through partnerships that share resources around common missions.

At the Southwest Cooperative, Dulle pulled 92 districts together to create a special-education professional development co-op. At UCP Greater Chicago, he organized districts across Illinois to form Infinitec, originally an assistive technology loan library, but later expanded to provide professional development to educators along with numerous other equipment and professional supports that benefit more than a million learners in five states.

So it seemed natural for Dulle to take the leadership of ERDI when founder Mike Kneale's health failed. In its 30-year existence, ERDI has never advertised or marketed. Its strong reputation and continued success are the results of word of mouth alone. The institute brings together public-school superintendents and education companies to discuss what school districts need, what companies can provide, and how they can all work together toward that end. Dulle noted, "There are lots and lots of excellent resources beyond what we presently use in our districts. ERDI superintendents are exceptional leaders who are eager to dialogue, listen to new ideas, and learn about quality products, goods, and services that may prove beneficial to the learners they support. Unfortunately, sometimes it is easier for all of us in education to keep things going the way they have always been going, but ERDI and the superintendents who are integral to its success are deeply committed to bringing the very best to their staff and students."

Dulle continued: "ERDI has had a subtle but profound impact on public education. The definition of public education is obviously changing: the desks in a row, the agrarian calendar, building-based learning, and grading and evaluation systems are all slowly but surely being challenged. The next 10 years will see a great difference."

Dulle is certain that the 90 or so consulting educational leaders in ERDI are more aware and better prepared for the future because of the high level of conversations that occur between them as leaders and the companies that engage with them through the ERDI process. "Today, the flow of information sheds light on the vast array of products and services available to improve education. At ERDI, the dialogue isn't just one way. Everyone involved makes a contribution. The enlarged discussion enables both our superintendents and our corporate partners to create a better future together."

He explained: "ERDI has always had single focus and that is to bring quality educational leaders and committed corporate partners together to shape products, goods, and services for the K–12 space. No lobbying, no political influence. I see so many public dollars wasted because of the politics that surround education. When school district leaders and private companies work together, they can make a big difference. Ultimately that's a good thing for all learners" (personal communication, July 22, 2014).

DIVERSITY OF PERSPECTIVES: IT'S WHAT MAKES US GREAT

Alex Molnar is director of the Commercialism in Education Research Unit of the National Education Policy Center, housed at the University of Colorado at Boulder School of Education, and a long-term observer of commercial encroachment into public schooling by corporate America. Molnar finds little compelling evidence that privatization in general or contracting out in particular offers long-term benefits to schools or to the communities they serve. In addition to noting the lack of powerful supporting evidence, Molnar's criticism of private-sector engagement focuses on two broad areas: the political and the practical.

On the political side, he sees public schooling as subject to the same economic transformation that has shaped the American workforce since the 1970s, "a relentless shift in the share of wealth derived from gains in productivity away from labor and to management and capital." He sees the reduction of labor's percentage of the cost of public education as the objective of American business-led reform efforts, actualized in Molnar's view, through the replacement of teachers with technology, aides, and call centers. However, as Molnar sees it, reducing the costs associated with teaching will not save the taxpayers money. Taxpayer money will instead go to managers and, increasingly, investors—a scenario he predicts will lead to lower-quality, more unequal, and ultimately more costly public schools.

"The dominant contemporary education reforms broadly reflect the global embrace of market ideology," Molnar stated. He noted that American political figures have themselves become products of a sort and are now commonly described as brands in a political "marketplace" that is increasingly dominated by moneyed interests.

"Market ideologues with deep pockets are even reaching to school board elections, spending big and distorting the democratic process. It's no accident," according to Molnar, "that so many current reform efforts seek to minimize or eliminate altogether the public's control of public education through the political process." He concluded, "It is my judgment that at this point, mercantile culture is destroying our civic political culture."

In terms of practical measures, Molnar sees school superintendents as ill-equipped to manage PPPs, having neither the expertise to negotiate contracts nor the time or resources to properly oversee and enforce contract provisions. "While it's true that a bureaucracy costs money," he conceded, "it rarely costs as much as not having a bureaucracy to manage these affairs. Of course, the problem is that with cost of proper oversight, contracting out likely costs more than simply doing the work yourself."

Molnar is also concerned about the practical end game of privatization. "You quickly get to a very small vendor pool with expertise. Once the vendor pool is small the public loses whatever control of pricing it may once have had" (personal communication, July 16, 2014).

On the other end of the spectrum is Steve Pines, executive director of the Education Industry Association (EIA), a trade organization for education companies that was founded in 1990. A supporter of PPPs, Pines believes that one of the most important things an education company can do is to "be respectful of how darn hard it is to run successful schools. The daily grind of teachers and administrators is unglamorous and their service is performed in a political cauldron." In his view, education companies should never feel like the cavalry rushing in to save the day.

Pines sees substantial but uneven growth in PPPs between public schools and education companies and he's not shy about saying some companies should have been more true to their missions of serving children first. NCLB brought about dramatic growth of private providers in SES. But in his view, "the federal legislation, however noble in its mission for equitable access to after school tutoring, was forced onto school districts that felt a loss of control over providers inside their schools and how their Title I funds were spent."

Not only did the SES mandate garner the ire of public educators for having to use dollars in ways they didn't want to, SES also brought, in Pines' words, "a few opportunistic players entered the marketplace without the real chops in education and became a stain on the rest of the industry." To Pines, SES was "well-intentioned but soon became a flash point with many public school leaders objecting to the use of for-profit external providers."

Beyond SES, Pines cringes when a private company tells a public school that "We can do it better." It should not be seen as or feel like a failure for a public school to engage a private company for educational services. Companies have specialized services and capacities that schools can harness to meet specific objectives. Aligning interests in a PPP is key. Pines believes that schools aren't set up to consider or answer financial questions about the specific cost of an education function and are often at a loss of how to evaluate company X or company Y. He noted, "Being humble and being perceived as a solutions provider are important for private companies."

Unlike Molnar, Pines does not see PPPs as an erosion of democratic practices. "A public–private partnership is conducted in the furtherance of the public good and directed by the policy makers of the public good, notably school boards and their executive administrators." He admires "courageous superintendents who looked beyond the classroom walls for what was best for students." He also does not think that PPPs threaten teacher jobs. "Textbooks or math apps don't threaten jobs; they are not replacements for teachers. Computers were seen as a threat to teachers' jobs in the '90s and that has been proven wrong."

Pines sees the trajectory for PPPs increasing but not as rapidly as in the past decade. "Waivers [USDOE Secretary Arne] Duncan has provided most states have slowed the federal mandates that were drivers of PPPs." Nonetheless, PPPs will grow, in Pines' view. He noted, as verified by a 2014 study conducted by the Johns Hopkins Center for Research in Education Reform, that "Public school districts want a web-based list, a clearinghouse of vetted providers with references and pricing information where buyers would go which would also have fellow superintendents' opinions" (personal communication, July 9, 2014).

From Molnar to Pines, there is wide variance in opinions on how much private companies can or should actively participate in the delivery of services within public education. The stakes are high; some $630 billion flowed though K–12 schools in the 2010–2011 academic year. That's almost 7 percent of America's gross national product. Where does that money go? How large a slice is captured by private companies? Figure 2.1 provides a breakdown of K–12 expenditures into six big buckets, according to the USDOE's National Center for Education Statistics.

This must be the treasure chest that every for-profit pirate seeks: the low-hanging fruit that falls into the profiteers' hands through competitive bidding practices, RFPs, and PPPs. When those pirates follow the trail to "X marks the spot," they find that others have spoken for more than three-quarters of the treasure. Salaries and benefits command 80 percent of public education expenditures. With 18 percent, or $113 billion, going to services and supplies, anger about profits seems hollow.

Profit is corporate savings and what companies use to invest in new programs and improved practices. Just like individuals, businesses make decisions to put off things they would like to do, discipline themselves to use their money wisely, make judicious decisions, invest in the future

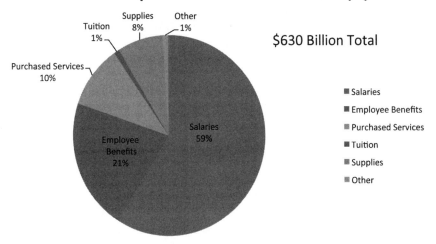

Current Expenditures for Public Schools (%)

$630 Billion Total

Tuition 1%
Supplies 8%
Other 1%
Purchased Services 10%
Salaries 59%
Employee Benefits 21%

- Salaries
- Employee Benefits
- Purchased Services
- Tuition
- Supplies
- Other

Figure 2.1.   Current Expenditures for Public Schools—2010–2011. Source: www.nces.ed.gov

without endangering the present, and save money (make a profit). After the profit is taxed, what remains can be held in the business, distributed to owners (or shareholders), shared through an employee ownership program, or given to charities.

The perception that for-profit companies in the K–12 education space do the least they can do to take the maximum profit home is far from the truth. With every PPP comes an obligation on the part of the private company to operate, to meet or exceed expectations, and to be accountable to a relationship in which it never has the upper hand. Beyond those relationship realities, private companies, unlike public schools, must make capital improvements, if necessary, through a general operating budget. Public-school facility development does not come out of a school's operating budget. There are differences between public-school accounting focused on accountability and private-enterprise accounting focused on profitability. But the difference does not equate to being wrong or caring more for money than children.

VIEWS FROM THE FIELD

David Bein, assistant superintendent of business services and chief school business official at East Maine School District 63 in Des Plaines, Illinois, appreciates what private companies can do. "School districts think in terms of savings. If a company comes to me and says, 'I can save you money,' I'm listening," Bein said. "I don't find a big conflict in for-profit versus non-profit. They both have a goal of doing good things for kids. I look at what is the best option for my district in the marketplace."

With a private sector background in mergers and acquisitions, Bein understands how the private sector can help his K–8 district's $50 million budget go further, but he's still a tough sell. "If we had a 1:1 teacher to student ratio, we could do amazing things for kids. But resources are an issue. Public–private partnerships may allow districts to meet students' needs and to do so with the most economic efficiency."

Bein likes getting involved in deciding about PPPs and thinks private companies should get the school business officer (SBO) in the process earlier, because sooner or later the SBO is going to be asked to weigh in on the decision. "While the special education director might be the point of sale," Bein remarked, "the special education [SPED] director is going to come to the school business officer. The private company needs to prepare an explanation of the value of its services to the district for the business officer or miss the opportunity. You need a good relationship with the SBO. The contract is there if things go badly; the relationship is the key. You hope you never have to go back to the contract" (personal communication, October 10, 2014).

In his eighth year as executive director of the Association of School Business Officials International (ASBO), John Musso has more than 30 years of experience with PPPs. "The concept behind PPPs was evident in the 1980s and 1990s, before they were called PPPs," Musso said. For example, Musso was instrumental in creating a technical academy within a B. F. Goodrich facility for the Pueblo School District in Colorado. The site created "an incubator, a new concept for alternative methods of learning/hands-on learning for all types of students," he recalled.

"School business officials are poised for more PPPs," Musso opined. "If a school district isn't able to provide the service, I see nothing wrong with the district hiring someone to help them provide that service, as long as the PPP has a strong business plan poised for success. A PPP is a business agreement, but without shared vision it won't work. When it does work, what the district, community, and students get out of a PPP is usually invaluable. A good PPP creates opportunities for students, improves outcomes, maximizes cost benefits, and increases enrollment."

When it comes to PPPs in special education, Musso noted, "I'm passionate about this. Put the expense aside. Let's talk about the child. Schools try to provide what they can, but at some point they don't have the staff or other resources to accomplish this task. This is not an administrative failure. I'm a generalist. The district is a generalist. It can't always provide the level of care needed for some children."

In 2008, ASBO sponsored a special conference on PPPs. "Individuals from the National Council for Public–Private Partnerships attended, as well as other experts and practitioners," Musso explained. "Those basic tenets for entering a PPP in the early 1980s still hold true today."

Musso reflected on the evolution under way with regard to the position of a school business official. "I'm the last of a dying breed," he mused. "I came up through the ranks as a teacher, school principal, then on to CFO. Today we are seeing second-career people with an acumen of business experience coming to the profession—bankers, accountants, CPAs, and other business and finance professionals. What these individuals bring to the profession is invaluable relative to business perspectives and, in most cases, they are keenly aware of the benefits of PPPs. And, as with the school business official of old, the newer SBO is focused on student achievement and making a difference in public education" (personal communication, October 20, 2014).

With more than 30 years as a superintendent for three school districts, Steve Joel has led Nebraska's Lincoln Public Schools for the past five years. Joel is a strong believer that PPPs help get the job done for his 38,000 students and allow him to do more with his $340 million budget. His longevity adds to his perspective. Joel remarked, "We did a good job until some 15 years ago, then special education, immigration, and new rules and expectations weighed us down. While it's incumbent on us to figure it out ourselves, we can't do it alone. Private companies save public schools a ton of time to create, develop, and implement. It is far more efficient for taxpayers."

He continued, "Unless a superintendent is driven by personal ego, he or she is looking for partners. By far, word-of-mouth is the most powerful marketing tool a business can have. I just returned from the League of Innovative Schools and superintendents were talking about partners. Mass marketing materials or emails don't work, but word-of-mouth about a program that blew through expectations is the best you can get to grow regionally or nationally."

For Joel, PPPs are best when they fit into a strategic plan. "Over the years, a strategic plan can drive a lot of the public–private partnerships. A $500,000 deal with experts brings a lot of scrutiny. It takes three to six months from the introduction of an idea to approval. But if I believe in the value, I move forward even if it's a tough political sell. I have to show where the funds are coming from and show one-, three-, and five-year sustainability. It's never cheaper to go out and hire new people. We just can't keep hiring people to experiment. I'd rather have a three-to five-year contract to fulfill a special purpose. I look for partners who wear the responsibility as heavily as we do. I want a partner who picks up the phone and calls me when bad news happens before I call him."

Joel continued, "Over 30 years, for-profit versus non-profit has been a nonissue. A reasonable cost and results are what matter. We have two to three dozen nonprofits working with the Lincoln Public Schools and we couldn't do without them. But creating something we can't produce ourselves, that's not what nonprofits do. That is done by companies with capital, skills, and expertise" (personal communication, October 13, 2014).

DÉJÀ VU OR VUJA DE?

In his 2014 book, *A More Beautiful Question: The Power of Inquiry to Spark Breakthrough Ideas*, Warren Berger argued that one of the most powerful forces for igniting change is asking the right question. Here's a portion of what Berger offered on the idea of *vuja de*:

> Upon stepping back and reexamining something you've been looking at the same way for years, you might suddenly feel as if you're seeing it for the first time.
>
> If you've ever experienced this, it feels a bit like déjà vu in reverse. With déjà vu, you go somewhere you've never before been yet it seems oddly familiar; conversely, when you look at something familiar and suddenly see it fresh, this is a case of *vuja de*, to use a quirky term favored by Stanford University professor and author Bob Sutton.
>
> Sutton has argued that if we train ourselves to look at the world around us through a *vuja de* lens, it can open us to a range of new possibilities—fresh questions to ask, ideas to pursue, challenges to tackle, all previously unnoticed because they were camouflaged in overly familiar surroundings. Adopting this view, business leaders and managers are more apt to notice inconsistencies and outdated methods—as well as dormant opportunities. Someone working on social issues or even personal ones is likely to notice more and to ask fundamental questions about what he or she notices. (Berger 2014, 84)

In 2003, something happened in South Dakota that had not happened in more than 50 years: a new public-school district was formed. It was a blank-slate moment. The inaugural school board had the opportunity to create a district like no other in the state. It could think creatively on every aspect of the district: facilities, personnel, curriculum, structure, organization, technology. Forward-thinking members of the community invited national experts to encourage the new board to use the opportunity to create a world-class school district, learning from the rapid advances and changes in so many ways that were transpiring in schools coast to coast. The school board members chose instead to replicate their grandfathers' district.

The replication of the schools they had attended and their parents had attended was comfortable and familiar. The *vuja de* opportunity resulted in *déjà vu*. It's understandable to an extent. Those school board members were chosen to pull a district out of the ground, to be good stewards of the public's trust and the public's money. None of them were education experts. All of them labored tirelessly and did their public service. And that's part of the problem, part of the reason public schooling repeats itself so often without asking beautiful questions or doing such things as embracing PPPs that advance the students and the community further and faster. Old perspectives often miss new opportunities. But school boards are stewards of the public trust, not askers of beautiful questions.

Reed Hastings asked a beautiful question. Frustrated with the late fees he was charged for rentals at the video store, he wondered why he had to pay late fees. When his homemade cardboard sleeves with DVDs intact made their way through the U.S. Postal Service back to his mailbox, Netflix was born.

Hastings spoke at the Arizona State University–Global Silicon Valley Education Innovation Summit in Scottsdale, Arizona, in April 2014. Calling school districts "parochial, byzantine, and difficult to sell to," Hastings articulated in his keynote address the main reason private companies struggle in offering valid, efficient, and effective services to school districts. He noted that public schools' greatest handicap is the changing of elected school boards and the rotation of superintendents. This transience at the top makes long-term planning and stability for public-school districts wholly elusive.

By Hastings' observation, public schools uniquely suffer from this problem within our country. Corporations, churches, nonprofits, universities, the U.S. military branches, and all significant organizations in our country have self-perpetuating boards and smooth transitions of leaders that provide consistency and constancy to the organization. Not so in public-school districts, where the average stay of an urban superintendent is three years: a year for a honeymoon, a year to offend a key constituency, and a year to look for a new job. With so much transience at the top, just who's in charge of public education?

DON'T BLAME US, WE'RE JUST THE TEACHERS

The difference in the involvement of private companies in the class-room compared to the lunchroom can be partially explained by the lack of *vuja de* experiences among school leaders, a parochial perspective, a comfort with the past, and a hesitancy to see things differently. But can it also be partially explained by the realities of organized labor? More than three-quarters of public-school teachers belong to a union and of those, just over 60 percent are covered under collective bargaining (Moe 2011).

Before 1960, few teachers were covered under collective bargaining agreements. By 1965, approximately 10 percent were covered; about 50 percent were covered under collective bargaining by 1975. By the late 1970s and until today, the percentage of teachers covered under collective bargaining has hovered in the low '60s (Moe 2011). The unionization of teachers was a solution to the problem of their mistreatment. Indeed, unionization protected teachers from patronization, nepotism, and unfair dismissal; it elevated salaries from charitable levels to solid middle-class earnings and has given teachers a substantial voice in their working conditions.

But in an environment with transience among superintendents and school board members, the teachers have put down roots. According to Moe:

> It is a fact that the teachers unions have vested interests in preserv-ing the existing education system, regardless of how poorly it per-forms. It is a fact that they are more powerful—by far—than any other groups involved in the politics of education. And it is a fact that, in a government of checks and balances, they can use their power to block or weaken most reforms they do not like. To recog-nize as much is not to launch ideological attacks against the unions. It is simply to recognize the political world as it is. (Moe 2011, 340)

But, with acknowledgment of the organized nature of most teachers in the United States, and with all due respect, teachers don't engage in

PPPs on behalf of the school district; superintendents lead that activity with approval of the school board. Teachers are substantially down the list of obstacles to PPPs, especially those who teach at-risk students, at least in the experience of Educational Services of America. So why don't administrators more frequently embrace private companies as a tool to meet the needs of the students? There are a number of possibilities, but one rises to the top: a belief that the school district must do everything itself with public-school employees. Anything less is an admission of failure.

PRIDE AND PREJUDICE

Rob Brown is superintendent of the Jeff Davis County Schools in Hazlehurst, Georgia. In an earlier life, as the executive of high schools for the Douglas County Public Schools in the Atlanta metropolitan area, he frequently used PPPs to provide services for at-risk students. But Brown knows the realities of education politics and small-town living. He said of superintendents, "We're so territorial. This is my sandbox and I don't want you playing in it. A lot of superintendents worry that, 'If I partner with an outside entity, that means I can't do it as well as they can and I'm the education expert in this community'" (personal communication, September 4, 2014).

Brown's concerns are not far from those expressed by Brian Woods, superintendent of the 103,000-student Northside Independent School District in San Antonio, Texas. "When it comes to partnering with a for-profit company, that's an issue looked at with a lot of suspicion," he said (personal communication, September 12, 2014).

There is an unspoken but pervasive cultural element of public education. A vast majority of school superintendents have risen through the ranks. They have made their way to the peak position of their profession by succeeding at each step along the way: teacher, department chair, assistant principal, principal, assistant superintendent, superintendent. Their success speaks to the value of the institution they have served.

There is a brotherhood, a sisterhood, a tribalism in what they have accomplished, in how they see themselves, and in their tacit agreement to perpetuate the system that has been so successful for them. In their leadership of a system that is under such attack, there is amazing pressure to keep public schools intact, self-sufficient, and independent of mechanisms that might precipitate its evolution.

There are other, less emotional reasons that might explain superintendents' reluctant response to opportunities to engage in PPPs to meet the needs of certain populations of students. Among them:

- A lack of experience with private companies. Many school leaders have never considered the private market to address student needs.
- A lack of private companies available. Some districts, particularly those in rural areas, may lack access to private companies.
- The enjoyment of the velvet handcuffs of the collective-bargaining agreement that administrators love to rail about yet live comfortably with.
- Statements from organizational leaders that cast a pall over the potential engagement with private companies.
- Funding systems in public schools that are so byzantine and divorced from function and outcomes that many school leaders are incapable of managing the dollars for specific functions and prescribed results.
- Lack of a *vuja de* opportunity for school leaders.

"In principle, it makes perfect sense for districts to try to take advantage of whatever the marketplace has to offer for its schools and kids. In practice, districts aren't allowed to do that. Powerful interests are threatened—and in the end, power calls the shots," according to Moe (2011, 340). Powerful interests may include superintendents' reputations, state departments of education, zoning laws, teacher contracts, racial politics, legal rulings, fund accounting mentalities, and cronyism.

The powerful interests that call the shots vary by location, and despite the reality that with their stability, teachers hold the balance of power, the percentage of unionized teachers does not explain at a state level the use of PPPs for special populations of students. California, with 96 percent of its teachers unionized, proves one of the toughest states to enter into a PPP with school districts to serve at-risk students, yet the state liberally uses PPPs to meet the needs of students with special needs. Texas, with 65 percent of its teachers in unions, rarely uses PPPs for at-risk or special-education services. Georgia, with 55 percent unionized teachers, liberally uses PPPs for at-risk students but rarely for special-education students.

Factors that either support or discourage the use of partnerships between public schools and education companies are varied and include such aspects as the state organization of education, population density, political leadership, and the cultural history of the region. These factors and others will be further examined in chapters 4–6.

It is a fact that millions of people and hundreds of thousands of companies make a living from public education. Which companies are welcomed to work with public schools and which are discouraged is a mishmash of attitudes and jurisdictions. As the next chapters show, the arenas of special education, behavior analysis for children with autism, and education for students at risk are areas where the expertise of private companies holds a great deal of promise for public schools and the children they serve if the regulatory, organizational, and cultural values allow.

REFERENCES

Band, J. 2013. The Changing Textbook Industry. Retrieved from http://www.project-disco.org/competition/112113-the-changing-textbook-industry/.

Berger, W. 2014. *A More Beautiful Question: The Power of Inquiry to Spark Breakthrough Ideas*. New York: Bloomsbury.

Domenech, D. 2014. Director's Corner. Retrieved from https://www.aasa.org/.

Education Research and Development Institute. 2014. Education Research and Development Institute. Retrieved from http://www.erdius.com/.

Moe, T. M. 2011. *Special Interest: Teachers Unions and America's Public Schools*. Washington, DC: Brookings Institution.

National School Boards Association. 1995, July. *Guidelines for Contracting with Private Providers for Educational Services*. Alexandria, VA: NSBA.

Publishers Weekly. 2013, July 19. "The World's 60 Largest Book Publishers, 2013." Retrieved from http://www.publishersweekly.com/pw/by-topic/industry-news/financial-reporting/article/58211-the-global-60-the-world-s-largest-book-publishers-2013.html.

Rose, M. 2014. *Why School? Reclaiming Education for All of Us*. New York: New Press.

Shapiro, A. 2013. *Education Under Siege: Frauds, Fads, Fantasies, and Fictions in Educational Reform*. Lanham, MD: Rowman & Littlefield Education.

Tienken, C. H., and Orlich, D. C. 2013. *The School Reform Landscape: Fraud, Myth, and Lies*. Lanham, MD: Rowman & Littlefield Education.

U.S. Department of Commerce Bureau of Economic Analysis. 2014, June 26. Personal Income and Outlays, May 2014. Retrieved from http://www.bea.gov/newsreleases/national/pi/pinewsrelease.htm.

United States Department of Education, Office of Inspector General. 2013. *Final Management Information Report: Fraud in Title I-funded Tutoring Programs* (Control Number: X42N0001). Retrieved from http://www2.ed.gov/about/offices/list/oig/auditreports/fy2013/x42n0001.pdf.

3

PROFILES OF PRIVATE PARTNERS

Things should be as simple as possible, but not simpler.
—Albert Einstein

A wide variety of companies partner with public schools in the areas of special education and the provision of education for students at risk. They range from companies with a national footprint to those that focus on a single metropolitan region. They include both for-profit and nonprofit organizations. The companies profiled in this chapter are only a small sample of the organizations that partner with public-school districts to serve students with special-education needs and/or those students who are at risk of school failure.

EDUCATIONAL SERVICES OF AMERICA

With headquarters in Nashville, Tennessee, ESA operates in 25 states. Founded in 1999 by Mark Claypool (coauthor of this book), who began his working career as a social worker and child-abuse investigator for the state of Tennessee, ESA has three divisions:

- Spectrum Schools and Programs operates 35 special-education schools and collaborative programs in California, Florida, and Tennessee. Spectrum began in 1977 and was acquired by ESA in 2004. (The fireworks that resulted from the acquisition are described in chapter 4.) Spectrum enrolls approximately 1,500 students with an average school size of just over 50 students. Spectrum employs 720 teachers and aides. A majority of the Spectrum schools are state-approved nonpublic schools (NPS) in California where it has PPPs with more than 200 districts. There are three schools in Florida under the Atlantis name that are parental-choice schools approved to accept McKay Scholars. In Tennessee, Spectrum acts as a direct contractor in PPPs with school districts. When Spectrum was acquired in 2004, autism was the most frequent primary handicapping condition served. In recent years, emotional disturbance has become the leading disability. Students within Spectrum are on a functional or academic track. The divisional office of Spectrum is located in San Pablo, California.

- Ombudsman Educational Services operates PPPs with public-school districts in 25 states for the provision of alternative education for students at risk. Ombudsman was founded in 1975 and was acquired by ESA in 2005. Ombudsman's blended-learning programs serve students in grades 5–12, with the majority focused on high-school students. In the 2013–2014 school year, Ombudsman operated 135 programs and educated over 14,000 students. The average enrollment period for an Ombudsman student is approximately 90 days. Ombudsman has enrolled more than 200,000 students. A blend of the Ombudsman and Spectrum programs called Ombudsman Plus serves public-school districts in need of alternative programming for high-school students with individualized education programs (IEPs). Ombudsman is corporately accredited by AdvancEd, and the divisional office for Ombudsman is located in Libertyville, Illinois.

- Early Autism Project (EAP) provides in-clinic and in-home applied behavior analysis (ABA) for children with autism. The company was established in 1997 and acquired by ESA in 2012. EAP operates in 11 states, with the bulk of its work focused on South Carolina and Georgia. Through its Education Alternatives brand, it partners with intermediary units in Pennsylvania to provide ABA for preschoolers and primary-school students. With the divisional office in Sumter, South Carolina, EAP employs 450 board-certified behavior analysts (BCBAs), therapists, and other professionals to serve some 800 children each week.

"All told," Claypool noted, "ESA employs 2,700 teachers, therapists, and other staff members to serve more than 17,000 children each year. When I started Educational Services of America, I had only the most optimistic hope that it would evolve to be the company it is today. Being the largest private K–12 education company is a small honor, like being the tallest short person or the biggest shrimp in the ocean. Despite inclusion on *Inc. Magazine*'s fastest-growing companies a number of times, ESA is still a small, privately held company.

"The company has a simple core belief: all children can learn. Whether it's a six-foot-nine, 250-pound emotionally disturbed 17-year-old or a 4-year-old trapped in his own world by autism, I believe, we believe, that those children can learn. That learning could be Algebra I, but more likely that learning will be self-control at a moment of anger or how to ask for a drink of water or tell a mother she's loved. When you educate tens of thousands of children and adolescents with special needs, you know that one size does not fit all and that each person's needs are unique. Addressing those unique needs is the job of Educational Services of America.

"The key to our ability to be successful with students is having strong relationships with the school districts with which we partner. Superintendents are the gatekeepers for us. They have tough jobs regardless of the size or location of the district. I am grateful there are a growing number of superintendents embracing public-private partnerships for some of their most challenging students, whether they are special-needs students, at-risk teens, or preschoolers with autism. There is certainly a place for specialists in the education arena" (personal communication, June 18, 2014).

SPECIALIZED EDUCATIONAL SERVICES, INC.

With more than 60 schools and programs currently serving 13 states and the District of Columbia, Specialized Educational Services, Inc. (SESI) offers public-school districts comprehensive and holistic educational programming for alternative- and special-education students. Founded in 1986 and headquartered in Yardley, Pennsylvania, SESI has built a reputation of providing specialized education services that allow qualifying students to avoid placement in more restrictive and costly residential therapy programs. Over its 28-year history, SESI has served approximately 100,000 students in partnership with some 600 school districts. The company's extensive array of service options includes, but is not limited to, the following models:

- Whole-School Model: a stand-alone school run by SESI staff for the partnering school district, enrolling IEP or non-IEP students with intensive special needs.
- In-School Model: delivers SESI's signature education model right on the premises of the partnering school, in classrooms designated for special-education or alternative-education students.
- Targeted Specialty Programs: meets the specific needs of individual school districts with both short-term and long-term solutions for the provision of (among other services) interim alternative education placement (IAEP) programming, off-campus suspension programs, life-skills and social-skills training, partial-day special-education programming, and credit recovery/drop-back-in services.
- Consultation and Training Services.

According to President and CEO Michael L. Kaufman, PhD, "There is an art and a science to what we do. The science part lies in the academics—in the learning process itself, in research-based approaches to adaptive education, in customized instruction for K–12 students with a variety of deficits, in skillfully implementing evidentiary behavior-modification techniques and incentives-based systems that actually change behavior. The art comes into play when building truly collaborative, effective partnerships with public-school districts, when creating a unified and shared mission. We're talking about the real futures of real kids here—you have to put a tremendous amount of time and energy into nurturing meaningful and genuine relationships with your educational partners to produce optimal outcomes for these students."

Kaufman continues, "Geography is paramount in terms of expanding SESI's ability to reach more students. We need to always know where the need is greatest, where we can make the most impact. To accomplish this, we follow the Office of Special Education Programs' (OSEP) 'Annual Report to Congress on the Implementation of IDEA (Individuals with Disabilities Education Act)' to identify which districts are favorable to working with privatized specialized education. We're looking for superintendents who 'get it,' who understand what is required for these select populations of students to experience success in school. It takes a lot of courage and commitment to the greater good for a superintendent to recognize that bringing in outside specialty companies can contribute greatly to fulfilling the vision for this district.

"In our most successful partnerships, SESI's particular expertise melds well with the district's particular expertise—we both bring something essential to the collaboration that neither could do nearly as well without the other. Districts want for their schools and students what everyone wants: satisfied parents, orderly campuses, challenged students working through their challenges, increased attendance, reduced suspensions, improved performance, grade-level advancement, and measurable positive results for students who learn better in alternate settings—this is what SESI offers" (personal communication, September 30, 2014).

CAMELOT EDUCATION

Camelot operates 35 schools in six states. Originally a residential healthcare company, in 2003 Camelot refocused exclusively on therapeutic and alternative day schools. Headquartered in Austin, Texas, Camelot offers four distinct school programs:

- Accelerated schools are designed for nondisruptive students who lack motivation. Students must be at least 16 years old to enroll. They are typically overage, undercredited, and at risk of dropping out. Accelerated schools are located in New Jersey, Illinois, Pennsylvania, and Colorado.
- Transitional schools focus on remedial, special education, and English as a Second Language (ESL) students who often display disruptive behavior. Life skills, vocational training, and computer-enhanced instruction along with counseling support services, community resource support network, and social services characterize this education approach. Transitional schools are located in New Jersey, Florida, Texas, and Pennsylvania.

- Therapeutic day schools serve students who are on the autism spectrum, may be orthopedically impaired, or may be developmentally delayed. The schools also serve children diagnosed as emotionally challenged or who have other disabilities that call for a special-education day program. Therapeutic day schools are located in Illinois and Pennsylvania.
- Turn around schools are in-district alternative school programs that follow the district's curriculum. The focus is on low-performing schools that want to enhance graduation and performance rates. Turn around schools are located in Pennsylvania.

CEO Todd Bock joined Camelot in its pivotal year of 2003. He noted that, "A good PPP is when Camelot is part of the district, embedded into the fabric of the district, included in in-services and board meetings. We like to be the silent partner with our success being the district's success."

With 800 chairs in its therapeutic schools, Bock is pleased that "a lot of districts understand the value proposition Camelot offers. With severely challenged students, we can give them the skills to keep them from being institutionalized for the rest of their lives." He appreciates when a school superintendent says, "This is your livelihood. Come help us."

Bock noted, "There's a place for partnerships with public schools. Private providers are not the answer but we are part of the solution. We're more nimble than public schools can be. We bring capital that the districts might not have that helps supplement public education" (personal communication, September 30, 2014).

COMMUNITIES IN SCHOOLS

Communities In Schools (CIS) was established in the 1970s by Bill Milliken, then a youth advocate in Atlanta, who had a vision for bringing community resources into public schools to assist at-risk students. As a nonprofit organization working with some 2,200 school sites, CIS positions site coordinators inside schools to assess students' needs and provide resources to help them succeed in the classroom and in life by partnering with local businesses, social-service agencies, health-care providers, and volunteers. The CIS national organization has a distinguished board of directors and partnerships with national organizations such as Feeding America and the Boys and Girls Clubs. The organization reaches more than 1.3 million students each year through a network of independent state and local CIS affiliates working in 26 states and the District of Columbia.

Today CIS is widely known and Milliken is respected by superintendents and business organizations from coast to coast. He served as the CIS national president until 2004 and is now the vice chairman of the board of directors. He recently received the Visionary Ambassador's Award from Usher's New Look Foundation; earlier he received the National Jefferson Award for Public Service, which is widely regarded as the "Nobel Prize" for outstanding community and public service. But it wasn't always so glorious for Milliken. He recalled, "I couldn't get a superintendent to meet with me for three years."

As a student, Milliken was asked to leave his high school because his teachers thought he couldn't handle the work. An undiagnosed learning disability caused him difficulty and he started getting into trouble until a Young Life mentor turned his life around. Milliken became involved in Young Life, an ecumenical organization, and said, "I was loved into change." He completed high school and what he calls "three freshman years of college" before deciding to move to Harlem in 1960 to work with homeless and addicted youth living on the streets of New York City. He "backed into" creating the Street Academies—storefront schools that combined social services with academic recovery for students who had already dropped out— the model that became Communities In Schools. Through an avalanche of hard knocks and his gift for community organization, Milliken understood that the community services that support at-risk students needed to be brought inside public schools.

What CIS addresses, Milliken said, "is not an education issue, but a response to a breakdown in communities. A vacuum developed between the end of World War II and the 1960s in which society and our faith communities changed. Schools fell into that vacuum. Schools built silos and safety nets but the steady flow of dropouts only increased. It took 35 years for someone to listen."

Late in life, Milliken got insight into his own learning differences. He said it "freed me up. I relearned how to learn. There are lots of me's out there and a lot of them are in prison." Milliken has written four books, the first of which was called *Tough Love*, a foundation for helping at-risk youth. "It's relationships, not programs that change people," he noted. "Love is the only transformative thing we have. My work went inside the public-education system because that was where the kids are, and the outside system was not sustainable. Relationships, love inside the school—miracle of miracles" (personal communication, October 21, 2014).

THE AUSTIN CENTERS FOR EXCEPTIONAL STUDENTS: A PPP IN THE SUN

As a public-school district director of special education, Francie Austin knew that many students in the Phoenix area were not getting an adequate chance. Along with her late husband, also a special-education director, they took a leap of faith in 1995 to create a private special-education school that would partner with districts in "The Valley of the Sun" to serve some of the districts' toughest emotionally disabled students. They opened with one student in September of that year and had an enrollment of 22 by Christmas. When they reached 55 students, Austin and her husband thought they had captured the entire market.

Today, the Austin Centers for Exceptional Students, known in the educational community as The ACES, operates three campuses in the Phoenix area and serves some 500 to 600 students at any one time and more than 850 students in an academic year. The schools serve students with emotional disabilities, intellectual disabilities, and autism while specializing in fostering appropriate behavior in students. Between 12,000 and 15,000 students have been enrolled at The ACES since it began.

The ACES is a classic entrepreneurial operation. Two special-education directors saw that a population of students was not being appropriately served. Those two people started a school and the need they saw was only a fraction of the need in The Valley of the Sun. The ACES currently serves 65 districts in the Phoenix area.

Austin has learned the "business" of special education with the growth of The ACES. It seems that once a district has a certain number of students enrolled at The ACES with similar handicapping conditions, the district creates a similar internal program and assimilates those students back into the district. However, Austin noted that many of those students will trickle back to The ACES because the district cannot replicate the positive behavior supports, motivational strategies, and the unconditional love found in The ACES educational environment. In addition, the districts are not able to demonstrate to parents the behavioral and academic progress that their students make at The ACES.

The Phoenix area is comprised of numerous districts that contract with The ACES. Austin is leery of taking her successful model up the road to Las Vegas where a single district is primarily responsible for providing services to children with exceptionalities. When a single district in the Phoenix area starts a program and takes students back from The ACES, there may be a temporary reduction of enrollment. If The ACES contracted with the Clark County Public Schools (Las Vegas) and the school district decided to create its own program, the impact of greatly reduced enrollment would be severe.

The ACES has established an important role in the provision of special education in the Phoenix area. Each year about 30 percent of its students are successfully transitioned to the districts and very few students need to return for a "refresher course." "It's not magic," Austin said. "It's extensive staff training, consistency, and a deep bag of effective techniques designed to reach students for whom most instructional methods have not been effective. We'll be around for a long time." Recently, Austin was called to the lobby to see a young man whom she immediately recognized as a former student. He was holding the hand of a squirming 7-year-old. "Mrs. Austin," he said while pointing to his son, "the teachers at The ACES saved my life and now I need your teachers to save him, because he's just like me."

Austin stated, "We don't look at this as a business; we look at it as a mission to turn the bleak futures of our students into futures of promise and potential" (personal communication, July 17, 2014).

SPEECH PATHOLOGY GROUP

Based in the San Francisco Bay Area, Susan Stark, CCC-SLP, formed the Speech Pathology Group (SPG) more than 25 years ago. SPG has partnerships with more than 40 school districts in Northern and Southern California. "SPG has close collaborative relationships with superintendents and special-education directors. By keeping current on state and federally mandated special-education laws and through offering frequent employee professional-development trainings on best practices, we have gained their trust and respect," Stark said.

The American Speech-Language-Hearing Association (ASHA) has more than 173,000 members; more than 142,000 of those members are speech-language pathologists (SLP). ASHA projects substantial growth for SLPs by the end of the decade. Among the reasons for that growth are increased survival rates of premature infants, improvements in the early identification of speech and language problems, increased school enrollment, and a growing need for contracted services by schools (www.asha.org).

Perhaps no other profession so tied to special education has evolved into an area of private practice than that of speech/language pathologists. (Occupational therapists and physical therapists come close, but those professions are more closely tied to the medical profession than to education.) The use of PPPs to serve public-school children with speech and language needs is not uncommon in many areas of the country, especially major metropolitan centers where a concentrated population allows private-practice SLPs to thrive. Many public-school districts simply cannot deliver the service components of an IEP involving speech/language development without partnerships with private companies.

But the PPPs in which Stark's company engages are not without risks and headaches. Staffing is a constant challenge. As the school year approaches, the number of children to be served combined with the variable of how many SLPs a district might have hired makes it difficult for a company to confirm job openings and make assignments that meet the district's needs as well as the professional and personal needs of its own staff. "It's like playing chess," Stark said, "there are a million moving pieces throughout the summer."

SPG is also aware of the business risk that is inherent in providing PPPs. Caseload numbers can decrease, or the district can decide to train staff and create its own specialty program(s) and/or directly hire SLPs, thus leaving the private provider in the lurch. "The district only needs to provide us with a 20 work-day termination notice. We have no guarantee that we will be asked to fill another position or help with additional caseload needs," Stark noted.

The district can also hire the private company's staff members, which is a constant threat to private companies. The private providers have not been able to get a noncompete clause (restricting the school district from hiring the company's employees) in the master contract that governs special education PPPs in California. Nonetheless, public-private partnerships for speech-language pathologists thrive. Stark shared, "Our local districts have come to rely on us to comply with a myriad of regulations and compliance issues. Companies are successful when they truly partner with the district" (personal communication, August 29, 2014).

ARC

As an after-school and experiential education provider, arc has PPPs with public elementary, middle, and high schools in Southern California. Headquartered in Los Angeles, arc serves between 35,000 and 40,000 students each school year. The for-profit company was started in 2001 by Gary Lipsky and Brad Lupien, two avid athletes and educators who wanted to bridge the opportunity gap for inner-city students.

Among arc's partnering districts are Los Angeles, San Diego, and Oceanside. Thus far, arc is primarily California-centric, funded by the U.S. Department of Education's (USDOE) 21st Century Community Learning Centers and After School Education and Safety grants. The company also serves private and charter schools as well as other community organizations, but public-school partnerships represent the largest portion of its business. "We have about 55 full-time and 320 part-time employees," noted Lupien.

The part-time employees are a combination of college students, coaches, and public-school teachers who work for arc after school hours. Programs include art, drama, tutoring, athletics, and a wide array of academic and experiential programs. At the high-school level, credit recovery is also offered. When a student has demonstrated needed proficiency during after-school credit-recovery classes, the school district issues credit.

Lupien's background as a former teacher helps melt icy relations that a for-profit company can receive. He observed, "Public schools can be extremely reticent to let a for-profit company come through the door. Once in the door, they see the value arc brings and they know they have an ally who will comply with the federal monitoring rules, who won't lose the grant for noncompliance. We overcome prejudice against proprietaries by our performance."

Arc's competitors are not the school districts themselves, but community nonprofit organizations. "I believe in checks and balances," Lupien said. "The for-profit nature of our organization brings business savvy and best product. We can charge less and we can do more, we have no other sources of support that allow for waste. In the end, our district partners see us as a for-profit with aligned values, flexibility, a great product that helps kids" (personal communication, October 8, 2014).

STE CONSULTANTS

STE is the quintessential board-certified behavior analysis consultancy to school districts. With 23 BCBAs, it is a major resource for school districts like Fremont Unified and Mount Diablo in the East Bay area of San Francisco. Sarah Trautman-Eslinger started the company in 2004 with an original focus on school districts. The company has morphed to include a substantial component of in-home intensive behavior therapy for children as young as 11 months.

The California autism insurance mandate, SB 946, "radically changed the landscape in our field," Trautman-Eslinger noted. "Insurance allows for better treatment with no age cap or dollar cap. IDEA mandates the minimum of FAPE. The medical model goes for the maximum benefit. It's been a wild 10 years, but the last two have changed the business completely."

Trautman-Eslinger described her group's approach to working with school districts: "We live and work in the school districts, in the communities we serve. We build capacity via training but more frequently we're called in for litigation or for extremely challenging children. STE can be the last stop before another nonpublic school or residential placement. We often serve as a bridge between the family and the school district in a difficult situation where there is finger pointing and there are accusations. We work collaboratively to bring the IEP team back together."

She explained, "About 90 percent of the services we provide in a PPP are conducted at the school with the remaining 10 percent in-home. Kids with autism won't pull themselves up by their bootstraps. It won't take care of itself. In fact, left untreated, it gets worse. Effective treatment means less treatment in the long run," Trautman-Eslinger stated. "We work with school districts to educate them because if we're all on the same train, we'll get there faster.

"School districts can hire BCBAs, but they must manage their case-load. Districts with BCBAs still have to engage STE. There are some 2,500 BCBAs in California, but there are more than 75,000 children eligible for services just under Medicaid alone."

Trautman-Eslinger's business is changing. More and more of her work is going through insurance companies and that is requiring greater administrative support. "Where five back office employees managed things in the past, 14 are needed now," she said. The growth of insurance-provided therapy as opposed to school-district consultancy is in full motion. "School districts and insurance companies—no one wants to go into anyone else's territory. At STE, we're doing less in the education field and more in managed care."

Trautman-Eslinger credited Lorri and Dan Unumb, attorneys for Autism Speaks, as major reasons for the change in her business. (The Unumbs are profiled in chapter 5.) She shared, "Dan and Lorri have significantly changed the autism landscape in this country. They are purposeful, intelligent, highly relationship driven, and are truly invested in the issues" (personal communication, October 22, 2014).

THE MAY INSTITUTE

Founded in 1955 by Dr. Jacques and Marie Anne May, the nonprofit May Institute began as a school for children with autism on Cape Cod. Two of the first students were the Mays' twin sons. Today the May Institute operates 160 programs for children and adults with autism and other special needs, serving families in 14 states. Among its operations, the institute has four schools for children with autism: three in Massachusetts and one in California. The May Institute also operates a school in Massachusetts for students with brain injuries.

"The goal of the May schools," noted president and CEO Lauren Solotar, "is to take the child to the maximum. Our schools have excellent educational programs in conjunction with excellent clinical services. Helping children reach their highest potential while working to return them to the public sector is what we do" (personal communication, November 13, 2014).

The two day schools in Massachusetts each have 24 students. One school operates a 1:1 pupil to teacher ratio while the other offers a 1:2 ratio. The autism program in Randolph, Massachusetts, the company's headquarter city, has a residential component with students living in seven homes integrated within the community. Residential students come mainly from the Northeast, but other parts of the country are represented as well. The Brain Injury School in Brockton, Massachusetts, enrolls 50 students, 20 of whom are day students and 30 who are residential. The Bay School in Santa Cruz, California, is a day program offering a 1:1 ratio, with approximately 45 students enrolled.

Executive Vice President Pamela Raymond is responsible for the oversight of these five schools. "The May Institute has resources that public schools just don't have. There are BCBAs in public schools, but the breadth of their responsibilities is great. When a student receives an IEP that specifies that a child needs these things, in this frequency, with this intensity, that is what May can do. Most schools like this in Massachusetts are full. It takes a long time to get a seat open. We recently accepted a child from Washington state but it might be months before a clinically appropriate bed is available," Raymond said (personal communication, November 12, 2014).

Solotar noted, "We help public-school districts directly through our consulting services. We provide best practices research with the goal of moving toward a lower level of care and heading to the mainstream." But still the May schools stand ready to accept students. As Solotar asked, "Can the education system infuse the resources necessary to provide the level of education and therapy that research indicates is needed for success?"

While the cost of the May Institute is substantial—1:1 day schooling is $105,000 annually—later treatment or inadequate treatment comes at a much higher price. A practical problem for the May Institute and for public-school systems is how long can and should a public district hold on to a child? As Solotar said, "If a child is held by the public school as long as possible, the public school refers an adolescent to the May with a longer and more ingrained learning history, who may present significantly more challenging behaviors and educational needs. In addition, many years of treatment and intervention during the most crucial years may be lost. Vast amounts of research indicate that early diagnosis and treatment offer the best prognosis."

Solotar noted, "The May Institute has a three-year plan for its education programs to expand to new areas of the country." She sees partnerships between public schools and programs like the May Institute as crucial, noting, "The whole system would improve if we worked together. We're working toward the same goal" (personal communication, November 13, 2014).

EDUCATION OPENS DOORS

In her second year in the classroom as a Teach For America teacher in Dallas, Jayda Batchelder had a realization: traditional content mastery alone does not adequately prepare students for postsecondary success. When 95 percent of middle-school at-risk students aspire to attend college yet only 8 percent obtain a bachelor's degree, there is a problem needing a solution.

Batchelder was by no means the first teacher to have that insight, but she is one of the few who created a business to address the problem. "Once I saw the gap in knowledge in my own students, I looked for a student-friendly how-to guide that compiled the basic information about the road to college. However, I couldn't find a viable tool, especially for first-generation college-goers," she recalled. "I put out a call to action to my Teacher For America colleagues in the Dallas area, and what we created was the building blocks of what is now the Roadmap to Success Program."

The Roadmap to Success Program is a response to the problem that Batchelder saw in her classroom and in her research: a step-by-step guide, a workbook, and a manual for students to use to understand the processes, the terminology, and the soft skills needed for postsecondary success, as well as a turnkey resource and program for teachers. The

200-page workbook is designed for grades 6–12 and emphasizes what Batchelder calls "college knowledge."

Batchelder knew that by creating her organization, Education Opens Doors, and continually revising the resource, she would be better able to scale the Roadmap to Success Program and empower students and families who needed it most. She had to leave the comfort of her classroom if she was going to affect more than the 140 middle-school students she had the opportunity to teach each day.

Education Opens Doors' mission is to empower students to navigate purposefully through high school to college. When founding the organization, the South Dakota native and Tulane graduate met with stakeholders and community leaders in the Dallas area whom she found to be receptive to innovative education reform initiatives. She quickly found benefactors who were willing to philanthropically support her in her endeavors.

In addition to the generosity of the Dallas community, Batchelder received the Texas Instruments 2012 Innovation in STEM Teaching Award, which provided her with a $5,000 prize that she used as seed capital to begin the organization. "The question of whether to form a for-profit or a nonprofit organization was answered through the generous support of the community," she said. "Although a large amount of our costs are subsidized by donations and grants, schools pay an incremental fee per student for the materials, which provides personal investment and accountability in the program. We chose this model based on our core values at Education Opens Doors, one of which is to minimize financial barriers and get these materials into the hands of the students who need it most."

The Dallas Independent School District is currently the largest partner for Education Opens Doors and the company remains Dallas-centric. As of fall 2014, 9,000 students have been engaged in the program across the Dallas-Fort Worth metroplex. Using a train-the-trainer model, Batchelder and three impact managers support 175 teachers to reach the 4,500 students enrolled during the 2013–2014 school year. "One rural superintendent contacted us with interest in the program, and now we're doing a virtual training and ongoing support for the program leader in that district," Batchelder noted. "We have more demand than we can currently meet. There continues to be a huge need for more instruction around soft skills. I believe that if we want to see change in education and fill these unmet needs, we have to continue to support innovative solutions in our schools" (personal communication, November 3, 2014).

AUTISM EXPRESSED

At the end of the first semester of the 2014–2015 school year, Michele McKeone resigned from her position as an autism support teacher with the School District of Philadelphia to go full time with the business she started in 2011, Autism Expressed, soon to be known as Digitability. Long before Facebook was a household word, McKeone studied social media at the University of the Arts in Philadelphia and saw the need for a digital literacy curriculum in public schools. Her journey to fulfill that need led to opening new worlds for students with autism and other intellectual disabilities.

"To understand public schooling from the grassroots, I entered the Teaching Fellows Program, a part of the New Teacher Project," McKeone recalled. "I took a position with the Philadelphia schools and was put in charge of a self-contained autism support classroom for 14- to 21-year-olds. This was the last stop for these students. I knew my students needed to be able to live in the digital world, use email, and navigate the Internet. I taught them everything I learned in art school."

The School District of Philadelphia liked what McKeone was doing and the Office of Special Services asked her to train special-education teachers. As McKeone taught her peers and presented at conferences, she saw the tremendous need for a curriculum for differently abled students to learn how to navigate the digital world and she determined to do something about it. She entered the business plan competition at the Corzo Center for the Creative Economy at the University of the Arts and won a $10,000 grant—seed money to start her business.

McKeone put her business plan into action by investing her seed money in her classroom. After further development of her ideas, she entered and won the 2013 Milken-Penn Graduate School of Education Business Plan Competition. The $20,000 award went to even further develop the product. "Digitability now has customers in public and private schools, day-hab centers, and lots of organizations that provide training services to the differently abled," McKeone noted.

She reflected on the route she has taken in the development of her business. "As an autism support teacher I was under the radar, I didn't get a lot of attention. That gave me a lot of authority and allowed me to adopt and embrace innovation and to be successful. It was a classic case of 'It's better to ask forgiveness than permission.'"

McKeone described her curriculum as "an online learning system that feels like a game to the students while teaching them word processing, Internet navigation, and presentation formats. The product makes learning possible for students who need a few more steps in breaking down the content. We're focused on Google, which is a one-stop shop. One password gives a student access to a blog, email, and word processing. Google is becoming the industry standard. With Autism Expressed, a student will learn the Google world and have a marketable skill" (personal communication, November 24, 2014).

WHERE THERE'S A NEED THERE'S A WAY

Companies with tools and services are ready to enter PPPs to meet the needs of students with special needs and those at risk. From proprietary groups with classroom-based programs that date back more than 40 years like Educational Services of America's Ombudsman, to nonprofit start-ups like Education Opens Doors, the private sector has responded to the needs of public schools. Providing the least restrictive environment or helping a first-generation student succeed in college, private companies can complement the strengths and core values of public education. Public education does not have to be the lone ranger.

REFERENCES

American Speech-Language-Hearing Association. Accessed August 2014. http://www.asha.org/.

4

PARTNERING FOR STUDENTS WITH SPECIAL NEEDS

A Well-Worn Trail (in Some States)

We make a living by what we get; we make a life by what we give.
—Winston Churchill

If a student in San Francisco is diagnosed with autism, with difficulties in verbal and nonverbal communications, echolalia, and repetitive patterns of behavior, and the student's mother takes a promotion to the Dallas office, will that same student be diagnosed with autism in Dallas? The answer is yes, it is highly likely that the student, if properly evaluated by professionals in San Francisco and Dallas, will receive a similar diagnosis.

Will that student receive the same IEP in the Dallas public schools as he did in the San Francisco public schools? Probably not. While the diagnosis of exceptionalities is shaped largely by the *Diagnostic and Statistical Manual V* (*DSM-V*), the determination of special education services is driven by the Code of Federal Regulations (CFR). States have flexibility to create eligibility criteria for services as long as they meet or exceed the requirements of the CFR. There is no guarantee of services or programs when a student moves with his or her family. When the IEP is rewritten in Dallas, it will be rewritten to provide the student with the services that Dallas can provide, not necessarily what he had in San Francisco.

There is no portability for an IEP. Parents who have fought hard for services for their children with a special need often feel place-bound, knowing that moving to a new school district for any reason would start the entire IEP process over. This is true not only for families moving from one state to another, but also from community to community within a state. There is not even intrastate portability for IEPs.

The disparity of special-education services in the United States is dramatic. The idea of a portable IEP has been met with doomsday responses. The IEP and the federal laws to guarantee an education for all students with a disability are trumped by state and local realities. The hypothetical example of a student moving from San Francisco to Dallas is offered to illustrate the wide variation found in special education across the nation. Among that wide variation is the use of PPPs to meet the needs of children with IEPs.

PRIVATE SPECIAL EDUCATION BY THE NUMBERS

Of the 50 million students in public education, approximately 15 percent—7.5 million students—have a handicapping condition and are educated under an IEP. Almost 100,000 students attend private placement schools—0.18 percent of all students in public education and approximately 1.48 percent of all students with an IEP. According to the *Digest of Education Statistics*, this percentage has held steady for the past 25 years. About 1.6 percent of students with IEPs were served in private special schools in 1989 (Greene and Winters 2007).

According to University of Arkansas professor Jay Greene, there is some resistance to the fundamental principle of providing a quality education for students with disabilities. "It's sloppy thinking," he said, that leads to worries that a private placement of a student will negatively impact mainstream programs. "Yes, some private placements are very expensive, but the number of students placed in such settings is small and school officials need to ask themselves how much it would have cost to keep that student in the district. There is resistance to the fundamental principle of IDEA. We as a society have committed to providing an education for all students and to allocating resources to do the job" (personal communication, July 24, 2014).

IDEA requires that a continuum of alternative placements and services exist in order to address the individual needs of students with disabilities. There are 6.6 million students with disabilities being served through IDEA. Of these students, "3.4 percent are being served in private specialized day and/or residential programs" (NAPSEC 2014).

The National Association of Private Special Education Centers (NAPSEC) member programs provide educational and therapeutic services to both publicly and privately placed individuals who are not able to be successfully educated in the regular school environment. These services also include infants and toddlers served by NAPSEC early-intervention service members as well as postsecondary college experience and adult living programs that serve individuals who have graduated or who are over 21 and are no longer eligible for services under IDEA. NAPSEC has more than 250 member schools in 30 states with almost 200 member programs located throughout the East Coast.

NAPSEC has seven states represented in its Council of Affiliated State Associations (CASA): Arizona, California, Illinois, Massachusetts, Maryland, New Jersey, and Virginia. The CASA adds an additional 400-plus members that fit under the NAPSEC umbrella of representation. NAPSEC is the only national association representing private special-education programs. NAPSEC's executive director and CEO, Sherry L. Kolbe, estimated that there are an additional 1,000 private programs serving special-needs students and adults in the United States that are not members of NAPSEC.

NAPSEC's primary purpose is to represent its member programs on legislative and regulatory matters coming out of Washington, D.C. The association offers additional services and has an accrediting body that was established especially to address the uniqueness of private specialized education programs.

The association also provides a free referral service for families who are searching for a private special-education placement. There is information on IDEA, IEPs, and due process issues on the NAPSEC website at the "For Parents" link. Kolbe stated, "IDEA is a comprehensive law, some 365 pages with accompanying regulations of 90-plus pages. NAPSEC provides clear information on IDEA for parents who have to work their way through a difficult system."

She added, "I think about all the families out there who are lost in the system. By the time they find us, they are at their wit's end searching for appropriate placements and services. The continuum of service is required by law for a reason; one size does not fit all. When parents are trying to get the best education and services for their son or daughter, they need to know what their rights are and what services are required by law. Knowledge is power in special education.

"NAPSEC member programs serve as a support for the public schools, in that they only serve students who cannot be served successfully in the regular education environment. It is not supposed to be an us-against-them mindset where it is a constant battle for dollars, but a system to provide appropriate services where needed. However, money will always have an impact on the system, unfortunately. When dollars are tight, my programs see a reduction in the number of students that are referred and in many instances, students are pulled back" (personal communication, September 24, 2014).

The challenge of providing an accurate description of the size, scope, and location of private special schools in the United States is a reflection of the 50 unique ways in which state governments interact with private education. An introductory statement to the USDOE's 2009 document *The State Regulation of Private Schools* sums it up nicely: "The contents illustrate the nation's ability to approach similar areas of education in a variety of ways. Not one of the states regulates private schools in exactly the same way as another. Rather, the statutes reflect the unique circumstances, concerns, and policy perspectives in each state" (USDOE 2009, 1). States range from aggressive in the regulation of private schools (e.g., California) to almost hands off (e.g., Alabama).

Professor Greene is "not troubled by variation from state-to-state in the application of special-education laws. The alternative is a heavier hand by the federal government, which would only make things worse. There is a high level of ambiguity regarding the regulations and ignorance by those implementing the law. I don't see any easy solutions to that."

Greene believes that IDEA and its predecessor, PL 94-142, were established on the wrong legal foundation. He said that the legal rationale that it was wrong to keep students out of schools because of race was used to contend that it was wrong to keep students out of schools because of handicaps. Special-education laws followed on civil rights laws. "Thus, we have a legal compliance model," Greene explained.

"Legal compliance models are very inefficient because it is so hard for families to access the courts, to hire attorneys, take time off of work, and so forth. School districts overwhelmingly win. They have the experts, the money, the attorneys, and they don't have to take time off work. The worst outcome of a legal battle for the school district is that it has to comply with the law."

Greene stated that civil rights laws were implemented to overcome an irrational hatred of African Americans. "The black customers who sat at the lunch counters were not refused service because they could not pay for a meal; they were refused service because of hatred. Schools don't have an irrational hatred of the disabled," he said. Nonetheless, the laws that have built today's special-education realities have created a compliance game of cat and mouse and dampened school districts' enthusiasm for creating programs for the differently abled. In fact, Greene believes that districts "fear being very good in a specific aspect of special education and having more and more families move into the community with their handicapped children to take advantage of the district's program. It gets to be a vicious cycle."

Greene suggested: "Instead of compelling schools to provide the appropriate services for a student with an IEP, give the kids a voucher of state and federal money. The IEP is an inefficient model. I would rather empower the parents to find the education they think their child needs. If students bring the money, schools will serve their needs" (personal communication, July 24, 2014).

Absent Greene's hope for special-education vouchers, the availability of private special schools and the differences in states' regulation of private schools are two explanations for the wide variation in the use of private special schools to serve students whose needs exceed the abilities of the public-school district. According to the USDOE's Office of Special Education Programs, five states place between 0.52 percent and 0.90 percent of their total enrollment within a private special-education school: New Jersey, New Hampshire, Rhode Island, Massachusetts, and Connecticut. Another 13 states place between 0.10 percent and 0.47 percent of their total enrollment in private special-education schools. That leaves 29 states that place less than .10 percent of their total enrollment in private special-education schools (Greene and Winters 2007).

It's worth noting that the District of Columbia Public School (DCPS) placed 3.03 percent of its total enrollment in private special-education schools in the 2003–2004 school year. DCPS experienced a number of class action lawsuits that resulted in almost one in four students with an IEP attending a private special-education school with more than $250 million spent yearly for those students' education and transportation.

While the percentages of children with IEPs placed in private special-school settings are less than 1 percent of total enrollment in all states, acknowledging the Washington, D.C., exception, there remains wide variation in the use of PPPs for students with handicapping conditions. For instance, New Jersey, with approximately 1.4 million public-school students, has more than 12,000 students in private special-education placements. North Carolina, with 1.5 million students attending public schools, enrolls 295 children in such settings. Rhode Island, with 142,000 students, places more than 1,300 children in private special schools, while Montana, with 142,000 students, uses private education services for 140 students. Massachusetts and Wisconsin have roughly equal student populations, but place 6,200 and 253 students, respectively, in private special schools (Greene and Winters 2007; NCES 2014).

Why the wide variation in similarly populated states? As noted above, population density and the availability of private providers are two reasons. Most students placed in private special-education settings are significantly handicapped. There has to be a critical mass of children with such handicapping conditions in relatively close proximity to support the development of private special schools. You could put 145 Rhode Islands inside Montana.

Further variation in the special education landscape is found in the special education voucher states. Ten states (Arizona, Florida, Georgia, Indiana, Louisiana, Mississippi, North Carolina, Ohio, Oklahoma, and Utah) have some form of voucher for students with an IEP (National Conference of State Legislatures 2014). While eight of the states' programs are limited by certain factors—for instance, Ohio's programs cover only students with autism, and several state programs use free or reduced lunch guidelines for eligibility—Florida's and Georgia's allow any student with an IEP to exit a public-school setting with a voucher applicable to an approved private school. No IEP meeting is required; the decision is a pure parental choice.

Florida, where the John McKay Scholarship Program (special-education voucher) began in the 2000–2001 school year, had 1,163 participating private schools serving almost 27,000 students with IEPs in the 2012–2013 school year. More than two-thirds of the McKay-eligible schools were religiously affiliated. McKay schools must be accredited but do not have to be exclusively for students with special needs. One half of the students who receive a McKay Scholarship in Florida qualify at Matrix 251, the smallest voucher amount and generally for students with a learning disability (Florida School Choice 2014).

If the hypothetical mom in San Francisco had moved with her son with autism to Daytona rather than Dallas, her son would not be eligible for the McKay program. He would need to be enrolled in a Florida public school and reported for funding purposes for the academic year prior to qualifying for the McKay Scholarship.

Jay Greene is pleased that 10 states have some form of special education voucher. "I'm not surprised that in less than two decades we have not expanded to national adoption. There will be a tipping point. We're not there yet" (personal communication, July 24, 2014).

In larger measure, the McKay Scholarship program and its brethren in the other nine states are state-administered PPPs. While the partnership is not written between a single private school and a public-school district, the state has created the vehicle whereby the private sector is achieving a public objective.

GEOGRAPHY AND BEYOND

Eighty percent of states do not have special-education vouchers; among those states without vouchers, the variation in use of PPPs in special education cannot be explained exclusively by geography. Texas, with more than 5.2 million students in public schools, enrolls less than 0.01 percent—fewer than 200 children—in private special-education settings. California is the third-largest state by square miles and the largest by population, with 37 million people and 6.3 million public-education students. The Golden State places 15,500, or 0.24 percent of its total enrollment, in private special-education settings. The states of Louisiana, New Mexico, and Georgia also place less than 0.01 percent of their total enrollment in private special-education schools (Greene and Winters 2007). While the use of PPPs in some states is a well-worn trail, in others there is hardly a trace of a path. At some point, the variation in the use of PPPs in special education can only be explained by culture.

Richie Ross has been a labor activist, political strategist, and lobbyist in California since the early 1970s. He attributes the active use of private special schools for public-school students with disabilities to "California's long-standing leadership in the area of disabilities." He explained, "More than 40 years ago, the political culture of California came to regard physical and mental disabilities as a civil rights issue. Part of the California culture is to honor diversity. A disability is just another form of diversity and in California people don't view looking out for the differently abled as the property of the education establishment. Equality is owned by the culture. California is intolerant of intolerance" (personal communication, July 10, 2014).

In general, access to public education came about through a series of court cases in the mid-twentieth century. *Brown v. Board of Education of Topeka* (1954), which ordered the desegregation of public schools, provided the legal rationale for access and services for differently abled students. Students with developmental disabilities won a key case for access in 1972 in *Mills v. Board of Education of the District of Columbia* that expanded access to public education to all children with handicapping conditions.

Public Law 94-142, the Education for All Handicapped Children Act (1975), cemented the right of all children with disabilities to a public-school education. It also addressed the placement of a student in a private special school. When no appropriate placement can be provided within the local public school, "special education and related services . . . including nonmedical care and room and board must be [provided] at no cost to the parents of the child" (Alexander and Alexander 1985). To this day, case law continues to define and refine the legal balance between public-school districts and the educational needs of a child with an exceptionality, including placement in a private or nonpublic school.

Mike Zatopa is a special education plaintiff's attorney who has represented families with children with exceptional needs for 33 years in northern California. He is a rare breed of lawyer who has devoted his entire career to special-education law. Zatopa estimates that there may be "a small group of attorneys like me in the U.S. and a huge number of law firms to represent school districts."

Zatopa noted that behind the federal cases that defined special-education regulations was the academic research of the 1950s and 1960s on learning disabilities and mental illness that led to better understanding of disabilities, coupled with affluent parents and emerging parent-lobbying organizations. In Zatopa's view, this evolution of a deeper understanding of exceptionalities led to a philosophical split between the states' criminal justice systems that see the behavior of exceptional children as free-will-based with stipulated punishments for violations, as opposed to at least the theoretical basis of special education that relies more on the understanding of behaviors as described in the *Diagnostic and Statistical Manual* and the clinical professions.

In addition, Zatopa's view is that school districts in more conservative states, such as Texas, or districts in states where budgets are very tight, will exclude disabled children from special education, focusing on the simplistic notion that children choose their behavior, even for children who have disabilities such as Attention Deficit Disorder or high-functioning autism. While he sees California as more clinically based regarding children's behavior, the recent budget crisis in California has moved school districts to revert to the simplistic view (personal communication, June 18, 2014).

Despite the regional variation in the use of PPPs to serve students with exceptionalities, an overview of students served in private placements illustrates the role private special-education schools play in public education. Students with a primary handicapping condition of emotional disturbance make up approximately 8 percent of students with a disability, yet they constitute 44 percent of private placements. Autism is the primary handicapping condition for some 2 percent of students with special needs, yet they make up 9 percent of students placed in private special schools at public expense (Greene and Marcus 2007).

THE MASSACHUSETTS MODEL

Where you live makes a difference, a great deal of difference, in terms of the services for children with handicapping conditions. Massachusetts might be one of the best states for special-education services and, not surprisingly, one of the best states for PPPs. But before it could create a positive environment for PPPs, Massachusetts had to address an old issue.

In 1875, Congress narrowly defeated an amendment to the U.S. Constitution proposed by Representative James Blaine of Maine that would prohibit the use of public money at sectarian schools. Nonetheless, many states passed similar laws and many newly forming states placed such language in their constitutions. Eventually, 38 states had laws or constitutional language, known today as Blaine Amendments, that prohibited the flow of public money to sectarian schools.

Massachusetts had such a provision, but in 1972 the state passed a law known as Chapter 766, which allows public-education funds to go to private schools to educate students with special needs. The law went into effect in 1974, a full year ahead of PL 94-142, the Education for All Handicapped Children Act.

Today, between 150 and 160 private-school programs, known as 766 Schools, are approved by the Massachusetts Department of Elementary and Secondary Education and the New England Association of Schools and Colleges. Two-thirds of these locations, which accept IEP students from Massachusetts public districts, are day schools, with the balance being residential programs.

Jim Major is the executive director of the Massachusetts Association of 766 Approved Private Schools (MAAPS). His group has 87 member organizations that operate more than 150 schools. Fewer than 10 private special schools in Massachusetts do not belong to MAAPS. Major noted that 5,322 students ages 6 to 21 were enrolled in MAAPS schools in the 2013–2014 school year. That number is 3.42 percent of all Massachusetts students with an IEP and .58 percent of Massachusetts' total K–12 enrollment.

Students with emotional challenges made up 30 percent of the enrollment. Students with autism accounted for 26 percent. No other handicapping condition made up more than 10 percent of the students enrolled in the MAAPS schools. Major reported that the average tuition for day students is $65,000 and $184,000 for residential students. While those numbers may sound high to many superintendents and special-education leaders outside New England, Major said that "MAAPS schools' cost structure is comparatively lower than those of public schools, in the neighborhood of one-third less."

Massachusetts has a long history of dedication to the differently abled. The Perkins School for the Blind and the Cotting School are examples of programs established in the early nineteenth century that demonstrated a concern for those with special needs. Major said the positive relations between the public and private sectors in the special-education arena "have to do with our history and very strong commitment to special education." He chairs a statewide coalition to fund special education. The coalition involves MAAPS schools, public schools, state leaders, parents, and advocacy organizations.

"There has been a massive shift in Massachusetts in the past 12 to 15 years," Major said. "Some 35,000 children have been diagnosed with autism and related neurological disabilities and there has been a concomitant drop in those diagnosed with a learning disability. The face of special education has changed dramatically because of the increase in the survival rate of pre-term and low birth-weight babies."

"Part C of IDEA [early intervention for infants and toddlers with disabilities] is a matter of routine in Massachusetts," Major noted. "Schools and health care do a really good job of identifying disabilities early." Major's two grandchildren, now in elementary school, had services from the day they were born with hearing loss. Today, both grandchildren have 504 plans and are not in special education. Major said, "The impact of the disabilities has been so minimized by the early services" (personal communication, July 28, 2014).

Massachusetts' early services for infants, toddlers, and pre-K children with disabilities are excellent and generally have a seamless transition to school district services. Major noted, "States are so short-sighted not to aggressively provide these services. It saves so much money" (personal communication, July 28, 2014).

Carla Jentz, executive director of the Massachusetts Administrators for Special Education, stated that "historically, Massachusetts has been committed to collaborative public and private efforts to serve students with disabilities: students with low-incidence disability needs are served in Massachusetts Education Collaboratives, and students with more complex disabilities are served in private approved special-education programs."

These efforts, according to Jentz, support the spirit and intent of IDEA for Massachusetts students with disabilities. She further stated, "Massachusetts LEAs [Local Educational Agency] strive to be educationally responsive and fiscally accountable, which is a challenge with dwindling resources at the district level and increased mandates." According to Jentz, the Massachusetts Administrators for Special Education collaborate with other organizations to advocate for the purpose of ensuring the best possible educational conditions for Massachusetts' students with disabilities.

"Trust is the most important element in serving our students," she said. "It takes trust between schools and parents to match student needs with appropriate programs." She credits the wisdom and foresight of the Massachusetts state legislature in leading the state in 1974 with the provision of Chapter 766 in creating a responsive public environment to serve the educational needs of students with disabilities (personal communication, September 15, 2014).

As executive director of the Massachusetts Association of School Superintendents, Tom Scott agrees that his state "has a social consciousness approach to children. If a kid needs a service, we have an obligation to provide it. It is what the state values. Districts will fight the marginal issues, but no one is going to fight if a legitimate candidate needs appropriate services. I see that across the board for our superintendents."

At the same time, Scott noted, "Many superintendents feel the procedural process is stacked against the public districts. While we all concur that the private special schools are good programs, district people feel that some kids should be at public schools. We have comparable programs to 766 Schools in public districts and in our inter-district collaborative programs, but districts are reluctant to fight because they'll have to pay the parent's attorney fees. The overriding issue is that we're all fighting for the same dollars."

Superintendents, in Scott's view, are sensitive to community relations. "What happens when we fight with a parent about keeping their child in the district, parents get vocal about the district not caring about special education and the parents are connected." He's also not convinced that 766 Schools save districts money, especially when transportation dollars are considered.

"The Massachusetts legislature created 766 Schools to address the needs for safeguards for special-needs students," Scott said. "A lot of state institutions were closed in the '70s and those students went to public schools, collaboratives, and private schools in response. The institutional support from the state essentially went away. Schools became the go-to places."

He noted, "I have never heard a superintendent complain about students who absorb too much money." Nonetheless, there can be community issues. "Parents, not school personnel, say, 'Why isn't my child getting special services?' This tends to pit families against one another. Spending $200,000 on one child has real local repercussions." Even so, Scott is proud of special education in his state. "Families move to Massachusetts for the level of special education services" (personal communication, September 25, 2014).

CALIFORNIA: WE WANT YOU; WE DON'T WANT YOU

Like Massachusetts, California was significantly ahead of the mandates that made special education a part of every school district in the nation. Where Massachusetts' head start centered on the state's storied history as an education and social-consciousness leader, California's jump-start came from aggressive educational and political leadership that blossomed after World War II. Richard C. Schnetzer was an active participant in the creation of California's current PPP environment in special education. Schnetzer took his first special-education position in California in 1968, having worked in the field previously in New Hampshire.

Schnetzer credits Marianne Frostig, Belle Dubnoff, and Aleen Agranowitz as the pioneers of special education in California. Each created a school for students with exceptionalities in the Los Angeles area in 1948, 1951, and 1955, respectively. By the 1960s, California had the Sedgwick Bill, which allowed county health officials to place children at private special schools and have the property tax revenue that would have followed the student to the public school redirected to the private school.

In the early 1970s, eight to ten private special-school leaders founded the California Association of Private Special Education Schools (CAPSES). In many regards, CAPSES was founded for the private sector to self-regulate rather than be regulated by the state, and it was just far enough ahead of the curve to succeed. As it grew, CAP-SES influenced the California Department of Education in developing its Master Plan for Special Education in response to PL 94-142, the Education of All Handicapped Children Act.

California's organization of private special-education providers paralleled developments in a few other states. In 1971, NAPSEC was founded. In its early years, many CAPSES members participated in NAPSEC, but eventually the number of California members dwindled. As Schnetzer related, "There is still a provincial element involved. The West Coast is far away from Washington, D.C., and most CAPSES members felt that NAPSEC and CASA, the NAPSEC association of state associations, were too East Coast–focused." The lack of California participation and the resulting Northeast focus of NAPSEC may have cost the rest of the states a mechanism to "establish a healthy private sector. The rest of the country missed out on something," Schnetzer reflected.

Schnetzer, who served as CAPSES president from 1983 to 1985 and then again 20 years later, is a realist about the relationship between CAPSES members and the public schools with whom they work. "The public agencies, at least a majority of them, wish we would go away. We're not very popular. There have been many local public-sector attempts to prevent new private special-education schools from opening."

In the early 1980s, CAPSES received funding to conduct a study comparing the cost of the delivery of special-education services in the public and private sectors. Schnetzer said that in his youth he felt that if the private sector could show that it costs less to provide the services, then the public sector "would beat a path to our door." But now, he said, "It is very difficult to compare the cost of private enterprise compared to public agencies." The facilities issue alone, which is a far greater burden for the private providers, is one of the significant factors that confound cost comparisons. In the end, Schnetzer believes neither cost nor performance rule the day. "It doesn't matter. It's public before private to serve these kids. The privates are seen as interlopers."

CAPSES, a 501(c)(3) organization, has more than 150 members, of which approximately 70 percent are nonprofit with the balance for-profit organizations. Schnetzer said, "This [PPP] works best when it's a dialogue with mutual respect. Many people on both sides have not taken the time to understand their counterpart. There are many private-sector people who have never been on a public-school campus. And only 20 percent of the time does a public-education administrator come to the private school. The turnover of personnel on both sides has this pattern repeated continually, which means we'll be redoing the same work in the vineyard. As intended by law, CAPSES schools are a safety valve to the public schools. Private special-school viability is made extremely difficult by a public policy which essentially says, 'We want you; we don't want you'" (personal communication, August 27, 2014).

With nearly 700,000 students, the Los Angeles Unified School District (LAUSD) is the second-largest district in the nation. For 18 years, Eileen Skone-Rees served as administrative coordinator for nonpublic services for LAUSD. It was a big job. Skone-Rees retired in 2012, but in her tenure as LAUSD's NPS czar, she overhauled the relationship with NPSs, often working hand-in-hand with Dick Schnetzer.

"LAUSD's 2012 budget for nonpublic schools was $115 million," Skone-Rees noted. That amount funded some 3,500 students at an average of more than $32,000 per child. When she assumed the role of administrative coordinator, LAUSD worked with 96 NPSs. That number shrank to 68 schools as Skone-Rees demanded that the NPSs "meet the standard of LAUSD as much as practical. For the most part, the NPSs rose to the occasion. When schools could not meet standards, we diminished the number of students referred and eventually the school disappeared."

Skone-Rees toured every NPS with which LAUSD contracted. "Some were so appalling that I would not offer a new contract, but I also saw fantastic schools, wonderful places for kids to be." When she took the position, she was shocked at the laxity and cronyism that characterized the district's use of NPS providers. LAUSD became a sophisticated and demanding purchaser of special-education services under her guidance, moving from a casual three-page contract to a contract of more than 100 pages accompanied by a procedural handbook. She demanded that an IEP be written before students were placed in an NPS or at the very least before the NPS was paid. "There was big pushback," she recalled, "I was certainly not popular.

"The LAUSD master contract became the model for the NPS master contract and was adopted by most of the special-education local plan areas (SELPAs) in the state. It set statewide standards and gave the California Department of Education an opportunity to use its enforcement as a tool to improve all NPSs in California," Skone-Rees added.

Skone-Rees teamed with Dick Schnetzer and CAPSES to address "the licensed children institutions (LCIs) (e.g., group homes) that were run on old habits that were offensive." It seemed that every child who lived in a group home also went to NPSs. Along with the California Department of Education, a study was conducted on providing quality education for children in LCIs. "This was important to LAUSD and members of CAPSES; we could not just abandon these kids," she noted.

In comparing Southern California with the middle part of the country, Skone-Rees said, "It is the lack of parent activism and the legal system that allow the middle part of the country to get away with doing so little. There is a cottage industry of special-education attorneys in California. Parent activism and attorneys [in other states] could blow things sky high. The change will happen for all the states that do not take the responsibility of special education seriously when the lawyers come calling on IDEA."

Skone-Rees recalled, "There are opportunities in LA not available to other districts because we are so large. LAUSD had 22 special-education centers." Combining district-run schools and the NPSs, there emerged "a marketplace—and a marketplace that was more evenhanded. We started a referral process where parents could review schools. Families with children with special needs had lots of choice."

Since her retirement, Skone-Rees has seen some part of her efforts dismantled and "people now in charge who do not understand the history." Like Dick Schnetzer, she sees people redoing the same work in the vineyards. "We are fighting the same fight because of people assigned to work with NPSs. The old ones are retiring and the new ones do not understand how we came to where we are. It diminishes the whole story" (personal communication, September 16 and 18, 2014).

Key in the interplay between public-school districts and NPSs in California are the SELPA directors. There are 1,100 school districts in the state and some 135 SELPA directors. Shelton Yip, SELPA director for the Napa Public Schools, noted, "In 1977, California was required to form geographical regions of sufficient size and scope to provide for all special-education service needs of children residing within the region's boundaries. The SELPA director's role is to ensure that there is a con-tinuum of appropriate services for students with disabilities."

Yip is positive about relations between SELPA directors and NPSs. "I believe that a majority of the directors have a positive relationship with many of the NPSs located within their boundaries. These are NPSs working closely with the district to meet the needs of the students and setting appropriate transition goals to return to the district" (personal communication, October 29, 2014).

TEXAS AND THE MIDDLE KINGDOMS

Stan Scheer was an assistant superintendent in Ferguson-Florissant, Missouri, before he took the superintendent position in Murrieta, Cali-fornia. He is now superintendent of the Thompson School District just south of Fort Collins, Colorado. While there's not a huge difference in the enrollments of the districts—Thompson has 16,000 students where Murrieta has 22,000—there is a huge difference in the availability of special education PPPs. "The big difference is the providers just aren't here in Colorado," Scheer said.

"In California we used SELPAs. My district wasn't big enough for a separate SELPA, but the SELPAs made me aware that we had profes-sional special-education providers for public–private partnerships. But even then, I was economically driven and I felt I could do more in-house. Parents of children with autism are organized as a group and are strong advocates for their children. Being the primary provider was key to keeping parents happy and fully vested. Over a three-year period, I transitioned a lot of services back to the district."

"But I have none of that here," Scheer said. "We are not nearly as sophisticated in terms of PPPs as we were in California. We do not have a critical mass of students with autism here in Thompson. But for those children with autism we do have, we have to find ways to be supportive and have services come through the school district. By having us do it, the district is more connected to the students and the parents in-home and in-school."

He added, "Nonetheless, we welcome PPPs when they are available. You've got to have tools in the toolbox. At times it's best to have a relationship with a private group that has the expertise we need. This stuff is complicated and we need consultants, advice, and services. We need to take the financial burden off the parents' back. I feel the pain of the parents when they come to the school district. We need to do even more than we have" (personal communication, September 9, 2014).

From her chair as deputy commissioner of the Tennessee Department of Education, Kathleen Airhart oversees many of the department's external relations. She knows the importance of advocacy groups. Prior to her appointment in January 2012, she was director of schools for the 11,000-student Putnam County (Tennessee) School System after serving as supervisor of special education. Airhart was the 2012 Tennessee Superintendent of the Year. She knows location is crucial for PPPs. "In Tennessee, we have some tiny, isolated school districts too far removed from the type of services that students need. It would be great to see more partnerships," she noted.

Before she led the special-education program in Putnam County, when she was still a special-education teacher, Airhart saw the long-term benefits of a determined parent who sued the district for services for his son with autism. "The lawsuit brought an autism program into Putnam County in 2001. As a result of the suit, the district sent teachers to the University of North Carolina's TEACCH Autism Program and to Florida State University's Center for Autism to learn about applied behavior analysis and develop a program for 3- to 5-year-olds. We also had staff from the FSU program come to Putnam County to help guide our early intervention effort. That program continued to grow and evolved to its current PK–12 program. The intention of the program was to serve the residents of Putnam County, but people moved from all over to enroll their children with autism in our program. It just happened. It was a win-win. We provided services and, with the additional resources from neighboring school districts that enrolled students, we could provide more and better services. The only downside was the district was identified by the state as having too many students with autism. Families were finding us for the quality of our program."

Airhart recalled, "Our allies in building that program were parent leaders in the community. The program that resulted from that lawsuit has helped hundreds, maybe approaching a thousand students over the years. Some of the most passionate work I have done has been figuring out how to serve children with severe disabilities. I know how much early intervention pays off in the long term. If we intervened early most students had significantly better outcomes by elementary school."

A lot of the work the Tennessee Department of Education does is the result of policy changes that require administration and regulation. Much of the improvement in special education comes out of the world of advocacy. "Advocates are a necessary component of making change. I have spent time with advocacy organizations to promote a partnership," she said. "It's a partnership that has to happen" (personal communication, November 11, 2014).

Brian Woods, superintendent of Northside Independent School District (NISD) in San Antonio, is no fan of PPPs in special education. His lack of enthusiasm is based on the scarcity of providers, a mistrust of the private sector, and a spirit of independence and individualism in Texas. "In Texas, you're going to have a broad variety of kids and you're going to have to serve them," Woods noted. "We're a large system and we serve all our students in both general ed and special ed. We spend lots of resources on our special-needs kids."

Northside enrolls 103,000 students and covers 355 square miles. "Some parts of the district look like New York City and some parts look like Montana. There are not a lot of options out there. There is one private provider in the county and a couple of churches that operate small programs. BCBAs are scarce in this part of the world," Woods said.

"We have lots of public–private partnerships with not-for-profits like Communities In Schools and the Boys and Girls Clubs. But working with a for-profit is an issue looked at with a lot of suspicion. The experience in Houston and Dallas of fly-by-night SES providers rings very loudly in the mind of Texas educators. That is brought up early and often when discussions about public–private partnerships come up. They ruined it for folks doing legitimately good work" (personal communication, September 12, 2014).

Yvonne Katz started her career in NISD as a special-education teacher years before PL 94-142. She was initially called a "crisis teacher" and was charged with "designing a program that would help special-needs kids succeed in schools. It took the true grit of a Southwest woman," she noted. "We had no resources. We had to develop everything ourselves. San Antonio is a military town and as a result of our work, parents with exceptional children from around the world were drawn to the Northside district."

That true grit served Katz over a 39-year career, almost 20 years as superintendent in Texas and Oregon and as an associate commissioner of the Texas Education Agency. Katz is dedicated to exceptional children but is tough and blunt when it comes to the Admission, Review, and Dismissal (ARD)/IEP process. "We have very strong advocacy groups and lawyers, but when the ARD/IEP group comes together and demonstrates that the students can be adequately served in the public district, that cuts off the argument that this kid needs a private residential setting."

Katz revealed, "The back story is that families can't deal with their children. They want them out and away from home. They want to visit them on Sundays. The public school is not responsible for the home situation but it is responsible for how the child performs at the public school. Attorneys and psychologists in the ARD/IEP meeting are consultants, they are not the law. It is the responsibility of the teacher and the principal to write the IEP and determine what is best for the student. Those who don't have rich special-education experience like me can be intimidated. You have to have your district people trained to not be intimidated by the lawyers.

"There has been a proliferation of autism. Autism is the label *de jure*. When I was a special-education director, psychologists would dance around and try to avoid labeling a child autistic. You don't have to be a BCBA to work with a student with a range of autistic behaviors. Texas is a combination of the *DSM* and *Crime and Punishment*. You look at the *DSM* and you look at the reality of the student" (personal communication, September 25, 2014).

The *Crime and Punishment* reference fits well with a study released in 2011 by the Council of State Governments Justice Center and the Public Policy Research Institute, Texas A&M University. In *Breaking Schools' Rules: A Statewide Study of How School Discipline Relates to Students' Success and Juvenile Justice Involvement*, researchers "examined the individual school records and school campus data pertaining to all seventh-grade public school students in Texas in 2000, 2001, and 2002. Second, the analysis of each student's records covered at least a six-year period, creating a statewide longitudinal study" (Fabelo et al. 2011, ix). Among the study's key findings: "Nearly three-quarters of the students who qualified for special education services during the study period were suspended or expelled at least once" (Fabelo et al. 2011, ix).

"We changed policy dramatically because of that study," said Florence Shapiro, who chaired the Texas Senate Education Committee from 2003 to 2013 and currently serves as chairman of Educate Texas and president of Texans for Education Reform. "That report was depressing. We knew things were going on but we didn't know how pervasive it was. We had a zero-tolerance policy that sounded good on paper but it morphed into violations for chewing gum in the hallway. That study provided us with the data we needed to change things. Enough was enough."

Shapiro is a strong advocate of PPPs and a proud Texan. "I'm a huge proponent of public–private partnerships in education. It is the only way we're going to have reform in public education today. As education chair, I learned very quickly that public-school leaders are so focused on their work day in and day out that they don't see that one of the opportunities that will help education reform is the merger of public and private interests. Public schools don't have the resources to do everything."

It is that focus on the day-to-day that can be a barrier to change, in Shapiro's view. "When you talk to people in the trenches, like a superintendent, they follow the status quo. The status quo is their best friend. They don't want people coming into their community saying, 'We can do it differently. We can do it better.' But the perspective that we don't need any help is just so absolutely wrong," she noted.

Shapiro understands the independence that Texas schools express and the pride they have in taking care of things themselves. "In 1993, when I joined the legislature, I found out the pride we had in our districts throughout Texas . . . rural and urban. We pride ourselves in Texas on local control. With 1,041 school districts, each has its own policies and programs. That's Texas independence. One size does not fit all in Texas. We're diverse in population, in demographics, in regions of this state."

Parents can be very vocal in Texas. Shapiro shared, "Recently parents stormed the Capitol demanding fewer state tests. That type of parental advocacy does happen here. But in a committee meeting to discuss a bill to allow children with autism to go to private schools, there was little parental support. Autism Speaks is a strong advocacy group but it is not very vocal on this issue. We need parents to advocate, to pound on the table to make services available. Many parents are just waiting. Unless there's an advocate, unless there's a hue and cry, there'll be no action."

Regarding more special education partnerships, Shapiro said, "It's a slow process in Texas, but it is a process. Twenty years ago, I would say we were stuck in the Little Red Schoolhouse. Today, through public–private partnerships, that is not the case anymore" (personal communication, November 7, 2014).

AN IMPERFECT LAW IMPERFECTLY APPLIED

Mike Kaufman, CEO of SESI, explained directly, "There are just some states that don't send out students. So unless something changes in those areas, companies like ours won't have a presence there." But he agrees with the superintendents who say relationships and total commitment are the basis for successful PPPs. "Relationship building is key. It's only going to work when we're in the public school side-by-side.

"Private companies can have strengths that work well with the district's strengths. We understand that the districts have certain resources and amenities that can attend to the student needs better than we can; and on the other side of that equation, we have a level of experience and program mastery with the particular populations we serve that can—and should—surpass what public schools normatively provide, which is necessarily designed primarily for a general population. It can be difficult for superintendents to let go of the belief that they can fulfill all needs for all students. Personally, I admire educational decision makers who can look past their worry that parents and students might prefer privatized options so they can see the bigger picture" (personal communication, September 30, 2014).

Camelot's Todd Bock shared, "SESI, Ombudsman, and Camelot help support the public-school mission, whether in special education or in specialized learning programs. A lot of school districts understand the value proposition these companies offer to raise academic performance and graduation rates. Our success is their success. But it is a challenge when your customer is also your competitor" (personal communication, September 30, 2014).

A successful PPP in special education comes from following the letter and the spirit of the law. As the assistant superintendent of business services and the chief business official of the East Maine School District in Des Plaines, Illinois, David Bein said of private placements for students with special needs: "I won't say, 'Oh no, we can't do that because we can't afford it.' If this, in the opinion of the team, is the best thing for the child, I say, 'Ok, let's do it'" (personal communication, October 10, 2014).

The Tenth Amendment guarantees that America will have 50 fiefdoms of public education. One federal law, IDEA, with 50 approaches, is a guarantee for inconsistency in what has proven to be a compliance model to guarantee a floor rather than a service model for maximum student benefit. Financial, organizational, regulatory, and cultural factors make for wide variation in special education and the use of PPPs to meet the needs of students with IEPs. As AASA's Dan Domenech noted, "The quality of programs has a lot to do with the zip code" (personal communication, September 9, 2014).

A successful PPP in special education operates in a culture of compliance in a district that seeks a portfolio of options, a district that wants what is best for its students and is responsive to parental and community advocacy. It is a partnership dedicated to implementing IEPs with best practices and jointly working with the many constituencies that comprise the special education arena.

But there have emerged two parallel processes in the implementation of special education: one for states that recognize a moral obligation to meet the needs of every student with an IEP and one for states that do the minimum. Special education is guided by a federal law that allows that wide variation. PPPs are adopted, adapted, or avoided to meet the needs of the local district. But, as illustrated in the next chapter, when it comes to children with autism, some of the basic assumptions in special education are being put to an unprecedented test.

REFERENCES

Alexander, K., and Alexander, D. M. 1985. *American Public School Law*. St. Paul: West Publishing.

Fabelo, T., Thompson, M. D., Plotkin, M., Carmichael, D., Marchbanks, M. P., and Booth, E. A. 2011. *Breaking Schools' Rules: A Statewide Study of How School Discipline Relates to Students' Success and Juvenile Justice Involvement.* New York: Council of State Government Justice Center.

Florida School Choice. 2014. McKay Scholarship Program. Retrieved from https://www.floridaschoolchoice.org/Information/McKay/files/Fast_Facts_McKay.pdf.

Greene, J., and Winters. M. 2007. *Debunking a Special Education Myth.* EducationNext, Spring 2007. Retrieved from EducationNext website: http://educationnext.org/debunking-a-special-education-myth/.

National Association of Private Special Education Centers. 2014. Private Specialized Education Programs. Retrieved from http://www.napsec.org/.

National Conference of State Legislators. 2014. Retrieved from http://www.ncsl.org/NCES.

U.S. Department of Education Office of Innovation and Improvement, Office of Non-Public Education. 2009. *State Regulation of Private Schools.* Retrieved from http://www2.ed.gov/admins/comm/choice/regprivschl/regprivschl.pdf.

5

YOUNG CHILDREN WITH AUTISM
Blazing a New Trail

Men are what their mothers made them.
—*Ralph Waldo Emerson*

History is full of mothers with total devotion to a son. St. Monica's continual prayers gave the Christian world St. Augustine. Olympia's shaped Alexander the Great. Sara Delano Roosevelt groomed FDR. But, as great as those mothers were in their devotion to their sons, they had nothing on Susan Butler.

In 1991, Butler gave birth to her first and only child, a son she named Collin. The first year of Collin's life was a textbook example of normal development. Trouble began, however, in month 14 when Collin became less social, slowed in his verbal development, and became interested in letters and numbers. Soon inconsolable tantrums began, social disconnecting increased, and an interest in letters became an obsession.

Butler sought help. A 90-minute assessment by a developmental pediatrician, a neurologist, and a speech therapist was inconclusive. There were signs of autism but not a diagnosis. The assessment team projected a grim future for Collin. Another neurologist spent two hours with Collin and saw him at his best and at his worst. Collin received a diagnosis of autism. Butler continued her mission to find the right treatment for her son regardless of the diagnosis.

Susan Butler's own mother, a teacher by profession, had served as a role model in demonstrating the tenacity needed to overcome challenges. Each evening she spent three to four hours supporting her son (Susan's brother) in overcoming a learning disability. Susan's brother graduated from Duke Medical School. "My mother was my example and I adopted her belief that children in special education don't stay in special education," Butler recalled. In Butler's hometown of Sumter, South Carolina, there was a model preschool inclusion program with eight typically developing students and eight developmentally delayed students, a regular-education teacher, a special-education teacher, and two aides. Collin was approved to join the program in February 1995.

But Collin's turning point was not found in the inclusion preschool. Despite Butler's engagement in the program and the full effort of the special-education teacher, Ann Eldridge, Collin's behavior deteriorated: tantrums grew worse; he obsessed on videos, movie studios, and spelling out words; his classmates steered clear of him, and teachers backed off when the problem behaviors arose. Ann Eldridge admitted, "We did not know how to teach Collin. I was a special-education teacher with a master's degree, but no training to prepare me for teaching Collin. Our class was innovative for its time, but I did not have the skills to reduce Collin's problem behavior or improve his language."

By fall 1995, Collin had regressed. He was more isolated and had made no language gains. The only glimpse of hope that Butler and Eldridge saw was that Collin, who would never comply with oral commands, would comply with directions if they were written. Oral commands were punishment for Collin. The fixation with letters and words placed Collin in the hyperlexic category, but he had very little functional verbal communication. Only through intense speech therapy and Butler's constant home treatment did Collin say "mommy" at age three.

With unending persistence in her search to help Collin, Butler learned about the research of Ivar Lovaas at UCLA utilizing ABA. His program seemed perfect for Collin. But, as Butler recalled, "you had to live in California just to get on the 12-month plus waiting list, and having just put our life savings of $5,000 to start my husband's business, moving was out of the question." Butler asked if there were other clinics that followed Lovaas' model. She learned that Dr. Glen Sallows had studied with Lovaas and was practicing in Madison, Wisconsin. She also learned that Sallows was not taking new patients.

Butler went to work calling Sallows' clinic, the Wisconsin Early Autism Project. Each time she called, Sallows was busy and was not accepting new patients. Butler kept calling. She got to know the women who answered the phone at the clinic very well. She chatted with them about Collin and about their children. She called 10 times. She called 15 times. She kept calling every few days knowing if she could just get 10 minutes on the phone with Sallows, he would want to see Collin. On her 63rd call, the receptionist at the Wisconsin Early Autism Project said that Sallows had just had a cancellation and she would ask him if he would speak with her. He did, and at the end of the 20-minute conversation, Butler asked Sallows to come to see Collin in Sumter, South Carolina. Sallows said he would think about it. Two days later he agreed and came to Sumter for a three-day workshop in Butler's living room.

Ann Eldridge, Collin's special-education teacher, went to Butler's home for the workshop, as did Butler's husband, her father, the newly hired ABA therapist, and Collin's speech therapist. The Butlers paid for everything. "It was really intense to go to a workshop led by Dr. Sallows," Eldridge said. "He is warm and funny, a doctor who cares about children and is sensitive to everyone in the family. In the field there are many who train from their desks. But Sallows got engaged. He trained the team to use reinforcement to encourage Collin to learn and taught them how to reduce problem behavior effectively. 'You never let problem behavior derail the treatment.' That was a huge surprise. You could actually make progress when a child was having a tantrum."

Before Sallows' visit to Sumter, Eldridge believed the problems were Collin-specific. "I never looked at myself and my lack of training. I felt I had nothing to learn from Dr. Sallows. But he is a brilliant man and in three days he assessed, evaluated, and developed a program for Collin and trained me, Susan, and the in-home therapist. Susan set up a 40-hour-a-week program for Collin and found the resources to bring Dr. Sallows back every other month for continued training. It was humbling, but Dr. Sallows made me see that I had been doing things wrong. Were we ever wrong!

"When Sallows came back to South Carolina," Eldridge continued, "he would observe me and if I was not running the program in the right way, Sallows would give me feedback or would change the training or the stimuli to increase the effectiveness of the program. Sallows would say, 'That was painful to watch. . . . Don't do it that way. . . . Your teaching procedure needs to change so Collin can learn. . . . Bad therapy is not better than no therapy. . . . A child's progress is dependent on those who are working with him,'" recalling the words of the master. "Dr. Sallows always looked to the teacher first if progress wasn't being made," Eldridge said.

Sallows returned to Sumter many weekends. He recommended that Collin leave the preschool and go to kindergarten with a shadow trained in ABA. Collin improved. Butler became the hub of autism activities in South Carolina. Families moved to Sumter to enroll their children in Eldridge's inclusion class. Eldridge was appointed to the Governor's Autism Task Force to improve public-school programs across the state. She also spent two summers in Wisconsin shadowing Dr. Sallows from dawn to dusk, soaking up ABA as he went from home to home, working with children with autism and their parents.

In 1997, on Ann Eldridge's back porch, she and Susan Butler had the exact same thought at the exact same time: "Let's set up a clinic in South Carolina." They left their jobs to start the South Carolina Early Autism Project (SCEAP). Eldridge reminisced, "All I wanted was to make as much money as I did as a teacher so that Billy (her late husband) would not have to say to me that 'You better go back to the school district'" (personal communication, September 5, 2014).

SCEAP grew. It covered the state with services. Butler worked with insurers and the state's Medicaid program. When Lorri Unumb, current vice president for state government affairs at Autism Speaks, moved to South Carolina, she contacted SCEAP to provide in-home ABA for her son, Ryan. Ryan's Law, mandating insurance coverage for autism, became law in South Carolina through the efforts of Unumb, other parents, and advocates, plus Butler and Eldridge. SCEAP expanded to Georgia, then to Florida. It employed dozens of BCBAs, hundreds of therapists, and saw several hundred children a week in their homes or in SCEAP clinics. Two women determined to help one boy created an enterprise that benefited a significant portion of the Southeast. In 2012, SCEAP was acquired by ESA.

The Susan Butler and Ann Eldridge story is remarkable. It shows the tender love of a mother and her absolute determination to get her son what he needed. It shows the courage of a special-education teacher to leave the security of her teaching position and dedicate herself to a treatment process that was little known, had an uncertain future, wasn't provided by schools, and wasn't covered by insurance—but she knew it helped children.

Butler's son did not have the grim future predicted at age three. He graduated from the University of South Carolina with a degree in linguistics and is fluent in a dozen languages (personal communication, September 5, 2014). But Butler and Eldridge's story is not unique. It has been repeated hundreds of times across the nation as parents, usually mothers, have created the programs their children needed but could not find in the public-school system. Maura Erwin created Educational Alternatives in Pennsylvania. David and Debbie Ide created Cornerstone in Indiana. Kristen Hudson started Growing Minds in Kentucky. Helen Schafer started the Schafer Center in New Jersey. Melinda Kotler and Michael Davin established the Magnolia Speech School in Pennsylvania. Karen Misher began A Step Up Academy in New Jersey. The list goes on.

Not only did determined parents create the right programs for their young children, a determined grandfather changed the landscape of autism forever. When Bob Wright's grandson was diagnosed with autism, Wright wanted to help. Like many people whose family is touched by the disorder, he learned all he could as quickly as he could and he was amazed by the scope of the problem. Wright learned that autism is treatable yet the capacity of health providers, insurers, and the schools to respond to his grandson's needs, let alone an autism epidemic, was pathetically unfit for the task. He and his wife, Suzanne, decided to start an organization in 2004. Being the former chairman and CEO of NBC put Wright in an excellent position to form the media juggernaut Autism Speaks, which quickly became a major force in the autism community.

Wright was outraged at the difficulties that were manifested in getting services for his grandson. He saw that what his family faced was only tougher for millions of families across the country that didn't have his resources. He noted, "I couldn't believe the ignorance and the unwillingness of school districts to partner with parents and insurance companies to deal with the treatment. I knew we had to prove through research that with early diagnosis and treatment, a child with autism could be indistinguishable within his peer group by the start of school." Autism Speaks poured tens of millions of dollars into building a research effort led by Dr. Geraldine Dawson, now at Duke University.

Autism Speaks also aggressively advocated for enactment of autism insurance reform laws requiring coverage of ABA at the state level and for increased federal research funding from Congress. The Wrights' organization has succeeded on both fronts. The evidence supporting the tremendous benefits of early diagnosis and treatment is rock solid and 37 states, plus the District of Columbia, have passed autism insurance legislation. Progress yes, but Wright's frustration with private insurers, school districts, and the political process is palpable.

"The battle has been won in 37 states," Wright said, "but it is a shame that we still have to pull out all the battle gear each time we champion legislation. Some states have had autism insurance mandates for years. Yet, we have to start the same thing all over again in a new state." Wright is also puzzled by the lack of support public education in general and superintendents groups in particular have shown in the fight for insurance coverage.

"There is every self-serving reason that boards of education should be out there partnering with Autism Speaks to get autism insurance coverage so that when the children come to school the problem of autism will be greatly reduced. Instead, school districts fight early diagnosis and treatment. They are just making it harder on themselves as they will be on the hook for the whole thing. The teachers' organizations have not fought alongside us. It's been parents and Autism Speaks."

Wright continued, "That's the oddest thing. Schools are so short-sighted. Had the schools and the education groups been engaged, we would have moved this much further. The dialogue between Autism Speaks and the public schools has been patchwork because schools are semi-political entities. It's hard to have meaningful discussion. Schools can do what they want. But the truth can't be ignored. Schools are clearly behind the eight ball" (personal communication, October 29, 2014).

One of the key members of the Autism Speaks team is Lorri Unumb. As vice president for state government affairs, Unumb has been deeply involved in state efforts to pass legislation guaranteeing that autism be covered by health-insurance programs. Indiana was the first state to enact such a law, and Unumb's home state of South Carolina became the second. Although a few toothless bills have been passed in the name of autism, such as in Alabama, most states have passed laws that require insurance companies to provide coverage for autism. All of the 37 laws require coverage for ABA. A few of them do not explicitly name ABA in the language of the statute, but they all require the coverage. Some of the laws have age caps and most have dollar caps for annual treatments, between $30,000 and $50,000.

One of the realities of the herculean effort to mandate coverage for autism is that it applies only to traditional health-insurance plans that are regulated by a state's insurance commissioner. Autism coverage is not mandated for companies that are self-insured, which is most companies with more than 200 employees. Those health-benefit programs are generally regulated under a state's department of labor. Along with repairing a few weak laws and getting the last 13 states on board, Unumb is also engaged in getting Fortune 500 companies to join firms like Eli Lilly, Ocean Spray, and Home Depot, which include autism coverage under their self-insured programs. For her tireless devotion to children with autism, Unumb received the NASCAR Betty Jane France Humanitarian Award in 2012.

The mother of a son with autism, Unumb had an aha moment in 2005 when she was writing a scholarly paper as a law professor. The paper was on problems and solutions regarding access to care for children with autism. The paper addressed the roles of families, schools, government services, and the medical community. But when Unumb stepped back and considered the environment, she noticed that health-insurance providers were not in the picture. Unumb related, "The health-insurance companies were doing everything they could not to be involved in any way." So she began to change things.

Unumb said, "It was not a school principal who diagnosed my son, it was a doctor. Why single out this diagnosis, why place all the responsibility on the school district? Autism is dynamic. You can overcome the deficits of autism by intensive treatment. Maximum improvement is possible. That's one reason I wanted the health-insurance companies involved. Schools must provide a minimum benefit, but people buy insurance so they can try to achieve maximum improvement. Legally there is not a maximizing standard in federal law governing special education."

There were other motivations for Unumb's actions as well. They range from the daily realities for families with a child with autism, to the administrative processes of special education, to poverty. "One phenomenon in autism is that the improvements are parent-driven. With autism you try to get through every day before you collapse. Families struggle to keep it together and couples struggle to keep their marriage together. Before Autism Speaks, there wasn't a strong voice for children with autism. Schools were getting away with benign neglect," she said.

"ABA undeniably works, but if you're not a wealthy family, you don't get access to it. I could not stomach that in the United States there are families with children with autism for which treatment is possible but who cannot access that treatment. The standard of care treatment was 100 percent not covered by insurance. I don't know of another disability or illness that has a treatment that works, but families can't access because of the lack of coverage by insurance companies."

The processes, regulations, and time drag involved with the implementation of IDEA are threats to children with autism, in Unumb's view. Autism is a health-care issue that requires appropriate and continual treatment until the potential of the child is realized. She asked, "To what extent are schools required to treat a health condition? Few superintendents have grappled with what a BCBA is or does. IDEA is not well suited for the needs of children with autism.

"IDEA was set against the context of the racist background that led to *Brown v. Board of Education of Topeka*. That same logic was applied to disabled kids. Those laws were designed to force a school district to build a ramp or buy Braille materials. Autism requires a completely different set of methods than schools provide. Our intention in IDEA was right, but our legislation doesn't work well for kids with autism. The law as it is sets up a system that is not workable. I would like to explore whether autism should have a separate law from IDEA. Right now we're placing square pegs into round holes" (personal communication, October 21, 2014).

Dan Unumb, Lorri's husband, is executive director of Autism Speaks Legal Resource Center and one of the nation's top thinkers on medical coverage for autism, especially Medicaid. In July 2014, the federal government issued a directive that Medicaid must cover medically necessary treatments for those with autism under the age of 21. Since that directive, Unumb has been engaged with numerous states as each works the federal guidance into its Medicaid program.

"We have Medicaid, IDEA Part C (birth to 3) and Part B, and private insurance all pointed at the problem," Unumb said. "There is tremendous variation in the quality of schools' programming for children with autism. Parents will frequently look to insurance reimbursed treatments first if they have that option because of the quality standards and provider qualifications. If parents don't have that option, they will look to IDEA and press the school for the highest quality Part C and Part B interventions they can get. But these—IDEA and health insurance—are two different systems with different requirements, purposes, and legal standards."

One of the challenges Unumb sees in the efforts to get appropriate service to children with autism via private insurance, Medicaid, and IDEA, is the standard of care that will be required by the funding source. Health insurance and Medicaid require a medical standard of care and will be likely to balk at paying for services delivered in schools that do not have the right personnel and institutional controls and are ultimately supervised by a school principal or special-education director. "Medical requirements are much more stringent. What is delivered under IDEA does not typically have to meet insurance standards," Unumb noted.

On the other hand, because of the stakes involved, "there is pressure on schools to provide the highest level of service for students with autism. This is truly a test to the system for what Free and Appropriate Public Education means for a self-injurious, noncommunicative child who is obsessed with spinning a plate, but who could recover from all that given appropriate interventions. The concept in *Rowley* (where in 1982 the U.S. Supreme Court ruled that schools had to provide only a basic floor of opportunity under PL 94-142) has no meaningful application for children with autism. Autism is a dynamic disability, not a static disability."

Unumb noted, "While there is great pressure on schools to provide the most effective level of service, the most efficient way of doing this, and better for the taxpayer, might be utilizing a private partnership. Schools have to take the child as they find the child. If the child has access to quality medical care, that's good for the child and good for the school. If the child does not have access to medical care, the school needs to recognize that it might not have the expertise to deal with the profound challenges faced by the child and that a private entity specializing in this may be able to provide services for that child more effectively and efficiently" (personal communication, November 6, 2014).

The arena of autism has changed so dramatically and so quickly that public education has been far more an onlooker than a participant in the process. Susan Butler and other warrior moms created autism treatment centers. Bob Wright launched a media juggernaut that has kept the spotlight on autism. An entire profession of behavior analysis has taken shape. Lorri Unumb determined that IDEA was not sufficient to address the full range of needs for children with autism and helped 37 states enact legislation requiring insurers to cover autism treatment, including ABA.

State departments of education are on the sideline of a movement focused on children who are historically in their domain. BCBAs are not credentialed through a teacher licensure program or via a state's department of education. BCBAs are credentialed under their own state professional-standards boards and occasionally under standards overseen by a state's board of psychologists.

In the past decade, the number of children on the autism spectrum has steadily climbed to its current benchmark of one in every 68 children, according to the Centers for Disease Control. No matter the reason for the dramatic increase, no matter the relationship between the increase in children diagnosed with autism and the change in the number of children diagnosed with other disabilities, the impact on public education is substantial and long-term. With the structure and the treatment of autism not fully in the hands of state-certified special-education teachers, and with an increasingly gray area of funding taking root with insurers and school districts both responsible for paying for behavioral therapy, PPPs between public schools seem destined to grow in the coming years.

Cristy Smith lives the realities of the changing environment of autism every day. Smith is the executive director of services for exceptional children for the Fulton County (Georgia) School District. She has nearly 10,000 students with IEPs in a district that is 80 miles from corner to corner; the Atlanta Public Schools cut her district in half. "BCBAs were not even on the radar a few years ago; now it's amazing how frequently they are requested," Smith noted.

Smith mused about the changes BCBAs have brought to her district: "I am fortunate to have two BCBAs on staff; they are hard to come by. District employees deliver early-childhood services in Fulton County, but I am forced to contract for services when I don't have a BCBA.

BCBAs are a budding parallel to SLPs, who we lose all the time to private practice. Private-practice SLPs are absolutely a safety valve for me. But districts can't treat them [BCBAs and SLPs] like beginning teachers with regard to pay or load their schedules with bus and cafeteria duty. These employees have unique professional licensure that warrants special consideration. They'll go into private practice and one of the places they go to is the legal arena. Many BCBAs have joined law firms to help parent attorneys. We have some very aggressive firms with BCBA support in Atlanta and strong advocacy organizations.

"The school districts in the Atlanta Metro area have the ability to deliver services that other areas of the state cannot offer. The GNETS [Georgia Network for Education and Therapeutic Supports] are a solution for autism and behavioral disorders but GNETS are state-funded and regulated agencies and not typically under school district control. The law mandates that a team comes together to decide what is best for a child, but GNETS can determine if the child is appropriate for the services they offer. School districts don't have that option."

The Georgia legislature has twice considered but has not passed an autism insurance mandate. If such a law passes in Georgia, Smith noted, "We are very curious about who will pay for services [schools or insurance companies]. Without insurance, parents will turn to the public schools where they have defined rights. We are going to be on the hook. It's a gray area and professional licensing may very well come into play, and that professional certificate [BCBA] is privately conceived.

"We don't do as much contracting with special-education companies compared to other large districts. We set goals for kids and I set a level of standards for Fulton County. How can I monitor that a private school is adhering to that standard of care? It is very difficult to do," Smith reflected. There is a stark reality for Smith as a special-education leader that resonates across the country. She noted, "The constant struggle creates a situation where districts are forced to rely on the minimum standards of the law more than we would like. No one went into this profession to give kids less than they need. But I have one pie that I have to slice and give the larger pieces to those who need it the most. We are forced to deliver free and appropriate, not always free and fantastic" (personal communication, September 9, 2014).

When it comes to school districts having a challenge hiring BCBAs, Billy Edwards understands. Edwards is a BCBA and a trifounder of

Behavioral Innovations, which provides ABA therapy for young children in nine clinics in Texas. He is now the director of the Center for Behavior Analysis at the Youth Learning Institute at Clemson University and the president of the South Carolina Association of Behavior Analysts.

Edwards noted, "When the programs and policies that shape special education came about, ABA was not recognized as a viable educational alternative. There were no board-certified behavior analysts until 2000. Most school districts aren't equipped to hire BCBAs, but if they would, the savings incurred would be substantial. Losing one or two mediation suits would more than pay for the employment of several BCBAs.

"While schools believe in local control, they won't add anything not sanctioned by the state's department of education," Edwards opined. It's the rare district in his view that is ahead of the curve when it comes to BCBAs. "School districts in the South in particular are very much against the notion of contracting out for special education. The attitude is, 'We're doing what we need to do and we don't need any help.' But even when special-education directors see the need for a specialist, they'd rather have that person in house rather than hire a contractor."

Nonetheless, Edwards has worked successfully with many school districts in the South. In his Texas days, Edwards was pivotal in shaping a multiyear BCBA training program with Plano Independent School District. "Plano is using the contract to build capacity so when the contract is complete, the district will have built the BCBA capacity it needs." In this contract, Behavioral Innovations is training the Plano special-education teachers in behavior analysis and provides the mandatory supervision to move the teachers toward certification," Edwards stated.

Edwards' other notable district interaction shows the potential for behavior analysis to move beyond working only with young children with autism. In fall 2014, Edwards and colleagues from Clemson took on the management of an alternative-education program for the Oconee County School District in South Carolina. He noted, "This program is not special-education-specific and these students do not all have IEPs, but I am writing behavioral programs for each of those students. If applied behavior analysis is recognized and utilized beyond students with autism and developmental delays, and if schools make career paths for behavior analysts, then ABA can help a much wider student base."

Whether serving at-risk adolescents or young children with autism, Edwards feels schools need to engage BCBAs. "There is an epidemic of autism, but I see kids now identified with autism who five years ago would have been labeled as ED. The effects are dramatic. Any medium-sized elementary school will now have 20 to 25 students with autism. But not enough schools recognize behavior analysis as a service option. This is now a procedural and organizational matter. The science is in. ABA works."

Referring to states that have mandated insurance coverage for autism, Edwards said, "Autism is the only diagnosis that comes with a supplement for an IEP in the public school districts." But that supplement doesn't just fall into the hands of the families that need it; it has to be built into a relationship between providers of autism services, schools, and insurance companies. The autism mandate had been law for more than two years before Edwards became the tip of the spear to put the law into action in Texas. That involved years of explaining ABA to insurance companies, negotiating rates, establishing billing codes, and agreeing to reporting procedures. "From my perspective, passing the law was the easy part," Edwards mused. "Implementing the law was the hard part."

Edwards believes a recent professional credential is likely to have ramifications for school districts in the not-too-distant future, noting, "In June of 2014, the Behavior Analysts Certification Board announced a new credential in response to the need for having a standard qualification for those delivering direct therapy. Unlike a speech-language pathologist, where the certified specialist delivers the therapy, a BCBA creates the treatment plan and supervises the service deliverer. The creation of the credential known as the Registered Behavior Technician will ultimately be adopted by state funders and insurers, and change the entire landscape of behaviorally based service provision" (personal communication, September 16 and October 8, 2014).

As a young profession, behavior analysis has made a rigorous certification process a foundational matter. When the teachers in Plano, Texas, finish their coursework, training, and supervised practice, they will still need to pass a professional examination to obtain national certification in behavior analysis. Gina Green is the executive director of the Association of Professional Behavior Analysts (APBA), a 501(c)(6) membership organization that advocates for the future of the discipline and its practitioners. The mission of the APBA is to advance and promote the science and practice of applied behavior analysis. Green has been involved in that science for more than 30 years.

The APBA's mission is closely tied to the interests of other organizations in the field of behavior analysis. The APBA works closely with the Behavior Analyst Certification Board (BACB), which is the professional credentialing organization for practitioners of behavior analysis. Because behavior analysis is a young discipline, a professional credentialing process that meets the highest standards is essential to gaining recognition within school districts and by governments and insurance companies. The BACB's certification programs are accredited by the National Commission on Certifying Agencies (NCCA) in Washington, D.C. The NCCA is the accreditation body of the Institute for Credentialing Excellence. Currently the BACB issues three credentials: Board Certified Behavior Analyst (BCBA) for professionals with master's or doctoral degrees; Board Certified Assistant Behavior Analyst (BCaBA) for professionals with bachelor's degrees who work under the supervision of BCBAs; and Registered Behavior Technician (RBT) for paraprofessionals with at least a high-school diploma, who must be supervised by BCBAs or BCaBAs.

These are new organizational names and acronyms for most public-school leaders, but they are likely to become more familiar as the incidence of autism continues to grow and as behavior analysts are increasingly recognized as the professionals best prepared not only to serve children with autism but also, in Green's words, "to improve functional skills and decrease problem behaviors in anyone. One of our goals is to get the education system to add the BACB certifications to their list of acceptable credentials."

The science of behavior analysis has a more solid research foundation than many methods teachers use in the classroom. Green said, "Many teacher-preparation programs are not training people in scientifically proven methods of teaching. And if we look at what public schools use for students with autism, most of it is ineffective, some of it is even harmful. ABA techniques are proven to work. Yet there is a lot of resistance. I haven't seen the education system having the capacity and the commitment to adopt techniques that help students—techniques that are proven by science. Public education has tended to reject rather than embrace and adopt interventions that have been proven effective" (personal communication, October 9, 2014).

Much as Rachel Carson's book *Silent Spring* lit a fuse for the environmental movement when it was published in 1962, *Let Me Hear Your Voice* did the same in 1993 for behavior analysis' ability to help children with autism. Its author, Catherine Maurice, had two children diagnosed with autism. After trying some bogus treatments, Maurice read about a 1987 study by Ivar Lovaas on early intensive ABA intervention for autism. Maurice and her husband hired a behavior analyst to work with their daughter, then their younger son. The story had a happy ending: both children improved so much with ABA that they lost the autism diagnoses and were in regular classrooms without specialized services by early elementary age. Her book recounts the family's journey. Green described *Let Me Hear Your Voice* as "compelling; it is hard to put it down. It popularized ABA to parents."

Public-school leaders across America feel the impact of Catherine Maurice's book. Add the wired nature and strong support network found among families with children with autism and superintendents know just how important it is to work effectively with them. "To date," Green noted, "only four state education systems have recognized BACB credentials in laws or rules: Connecticut, California, Louisiana, and New Jersey. The roles of BACB certificants in those states vary. For instance, in California, the education code states that schools can—but do not have to—hire BCBAs to serve as behavioral-intervention case managers for students with special needs. A law in Connecticut says that when a child with autism has ABA intervention in the IEP, that intervention must be overseen by a BCBA.

"The education system has its own set of laws and regulations," Green explained. "Just because a profession has a credentialing process, nothing requires an LEA to recognize it unless or until those credentials are added to the state education laws. As demand for ABA interventions for autism as well as treatment for traumatic brain injury and developmental delays increases, schools will have difficulty finding BCBAs. The profession is growing faster than we had hoped and I expect that to continue. Today there are about 18,000 Behavior Analyst Certification Board certificants worldwide" (personal communication, October 9, 2014).

WHAT IS PUBLIC EDUCATION TO DO?

Schools are to use evidence-based practices in serving all children. The National Professional Development Center (NPDC) on Autism Spectrum Disorders, funded by the USDOE, is "a multiuniversity center to promote the use of evidence-based practice for children and adolescents with autism spectrum disorders" (autismpdc.fpg.unc.edu). The various components of applied behavioral analysis such as discrete trial training, pivotal response, and many others demonstrate the greatest number of studies in evidence of their effectiveness. These are the tools employed by BCBAs, the professionals school districts struggle to employ.

PPPs are a lifeline to school districts to serve children with autism. Whether engaging companies like STE Consultants for training or taking advantage of consultation provided by BCBAs or placing a student with autism at a NPS like Spectrum or SESI where BCBAs design behavioral programs, public schools are in need of partnerships with autism specialists to comply with IDEA as it is written today.

Will the rule book change? Will a new law be written specifically to address autism? A great deal has happened in the past decade that addresses autism as a medical issue. There is great uncertainty as to whose responsibility it is to provide and pay for in-home behavioral therapy for a 3-year-old with autism—the school district via Part C of IDEA or the health-insurance company.

Ron Tomalis, the former secretary of education for the state of Pennsylvania, offered this insight as to how that might sort out. "When you do an analysis of what has the greatest impact on treating the child, that has the possibility of curing the disease or minimizing the disease, if the evidence is there that this is a curable situation, the money should go to who can provide the treatment. Schools will benefit by having children come to school who are cured or who have minimized difficulties."

But Tomalis thinks there will be challenges ahead. "If you redefine autism as a health issue, schools may very well lose the ability to tap into funds if they are not providing the direct service. Will the schools fight that change? I think they will" (personal communication, October 28, 2014).

The dynamic that Autism Speaks and Lorri Unumb created is similar to what happened in the 1950s, 1960s, and 1970s in California and Massachusetts: parental and legal advocacy to provide access to and to circumvent the "floor model" of public special education. Moving to a medical model is the antithesis of the kabuki dance of the IEP process. Speed counts in the treatment of young children with autism and the slow walk imbedded in special-education regulations costs precious time.

Parents are weary of the compliance model. They are tired of being gamed. They want evidence-based programs for their children with autism. They want to move the needle on their children's development. They reject the floor model. They want control of the process. They want a cure. They know that time matters. Early treatment is crucial. Teenagers with autism don't overcome the disease.

Divorcing the care of children with autism from public education is the canary in the coal mine. If responsibilities are shifted from schools to health providers, a money shift will follow. If autism breaks out of IDEA, will other handicapping conditions like emotional disturbance follow? Can it be argued that education itself is a behavioral treatment? There is an undeniable blurring of the line between health care and education that leads to the unavoidable conclusion that something is going to change.

REFERENCES

Carson, Rachel. 1962. *Silent Spring*. Boston: Houghton Mifflin Company.
Maurice, Catherine. 1993. *Let Me Hear Your Voice: A Family's Triumph over Autism*. New York: Alfred A. Knopf.
National Professional Development Center on Autism Spectrium Disorder. Accessed October 2014. http://autismpdc.fpg.unc.edu/about-npdc.

6

SERVING AT-RISK STUDENTS
Off-Trail Partnering

A popular government, without popular information, or the means of acquiring it, is but a Prologue to a Farce or a Tragedy; or, perhaps both. Knowledge will forever govern ignorance: And a people who mean to be their own Governors must arm themselves with the power which knowledge gives.
—James Madison

PPPs focused on at-risk students are not the norm, but there is good reasoning that they should be. While there are more than 10,000 district-operated alternative schools, there is no research on the number of PPPs in this area. Nonetheless, at-risk education is an area very suitable for partnerships between school districts and seasoned providers of education designed for students at risk. Before hearing from users and providers and examining some model PPPs in this area, it is important to elaborate on the concept of at-risk students: who they are, what makes them at risk, and what public schools offer in terms of alternative schooling.

CIRCUMSTANCES THAT CREATE AT-RISK STUDENTS

There are millions of children whose prospects for a good education and a drug-free, poverty-free, jail-free, hunger-free, violence-free life are dim. These children are found throughout the nation, but especially in areas of poverty. Despite decades of efforts to help them, despite programs offered in schools and communities, and through churches and nonprofit organizations, these children remain in peril from circumstances over which they have little control—and nearly all of these children receive their education from public schools.

Although students can be identified as being at risk earlier than fifth grade, most alternative-school efforts are focused on middle and senior high-school students. There are 31 million students in grades 5–12. Considering the long list of measures that could place a student at risk, the number of students who meet the at-risk profile is significant, though published estimates are few and vary by which subsets of at-risk students are studied.

A brief review of some of the reasons that students are at risk paints an astounding picture and frames the need to continue to address the education of these students despite the lack of a mandate such as found in special education. After all, a good education is the best opportunity a student has to overcome the reasons he or she is at risk, to break the cycle, and to improve chances for the next generation.

Food Insecurity

In 2012, more than 17 million households in the United States faced "food insecurity," which means those households did not always know where they would find their next meal (Coleman-Jensen, Nord, and Singh 2013). That's 14 percent of the nation's homes.

Almost 60 percent of America's hungry families participated in one or more of the nation's three major federal food assistance programs: Supplemental Nutrition Assistance Program (formerly the Food Stamp Program), the National School Lunch Program, and the Special Supplemental Nutrition Program for Women, Infants, and Children (Coleman-Jensen, Nord, and Singh 2013). Regardless, hunger stalks America. According to Map the Meal Gap, in 2011, the top five states with the highest rates of food-insecure children under 18 were New Mexico, the District of Columbia, Arizona, Oregon, and Georgia. Twenty percent or more of the child population in 38 states and D.C. lived in food-insecure households in 2011 (Feeding America 2014).

Poverty

Hunger and poverty go hand-in-hand. Almost 50 million people (15.1 percent of the population, up from 12.5 percent in 1997) lived in poverty in 2010, according to the U.S. Census Bureau. Just since 2009, 2.6 million more people have slipped below the poverty line. The Census Bureau states that 27.7 percent of blacks, 26.6 percent of Hispanics, and 22 percent of children under the age of 18 live in poverty. More than 20 million of America's poor live below 50 percent of the poverty line, meaning a family of four is surviving on less than $10,000 a year. More than half of Mississippi's school children live in poverty (U.S. Census Bureau, 2012).

Neglect and Abuse

Neglect and abuse trap children in a horrible cycle with psychological consequences that last a lifetime. According to the U.S. Department of Health and Human Services (2013), there were 686,000 children reported as abused or neglected in America in 2012. "Extensive research on the biology of stress now shows that healthy development can be derailed by excessive and prolonged activation of stress response systems in the body, with damaging effects on learning, behavior, and health across the lifespan" (National Scientific Council on the Developing Child 2005, 1). Abused children, along with society, pay a high price for these struggles in the form of poor cognitive development, substance abuse, risky behavior, and a high likelihood that the cycle of abuse will continue.

Sexual Exploitation

Sexual exploitation is a separate category of abuse. The number of children sexually abused is difficult to determine. The Centers for Disease Control and Prevention (2013) estimates that 24.7 percent of girls and 16 percent of boys have experienced sexual abuse. The Child Molestation Research and Prevention Institute (2014) states that more than 90 percent of the children know their abuser and a great deal of the abuses, perhaps half, are perpetrated by older children on younger children. Researchers estimate that as many as 20 percent of girls and

10 percent of boys are sexually molested by the time they reach age 13 (Child Molestation Research and Prevention Institute 2014). Estes and Weiner (2002) estimated that 310,000 American youth are at risk of becoming victims of commercial sexual exploitation.

Transience and Homelessness

The General Accounting Office estimates that there are more than 300,000 15- to 17-year-olds working in migrant agriculture and the United Farm Workers estimates that there are more than 800,000 farm-working children (cited in Human Rights Watch [2000]). These children usually work all daylight hours, seven days a week. The bounty of America's tables is too frequently picked by the hands of children who should be in school.

While it is difficult to estimate the number of people who are homeless in America, homelessness is a stark reality and affects many children. The National Coalition for the Homeless (2009) estimated that 3.5 million people experience homelessness in any single year. The National Center of Family Homelessness (2010) estimated that 1.6 million children experience homelessness each year.

Drug Abuse

In 1971, President Richard Nixon declared a war on drugs and named drug abuse public enemy number one. In the ensuing 40 years, America spent more than $2.5 trillion fighting drugs. Despite "Just Say No" and D.A.R.E. programs, drugs still wash across America. Despite crackdowns and tough sentencing resulting in almost 60 percent of inmates in federal prisons being there for drug-related offenses, the number of people who use illegal drugs in the country is at an all-time high. Joseph Califano Jr. (2010), former Secretary of Health, Education and Welfare, who led the Center on Addiction and Substance Abuse until 2010, said it was nothing short of child abuse for the government to require that children attend schools that are rampant with drugs and gang activity.

Incarceration

According to the Children's Defense Fund (2012), on any given day, approximately 81,000 children are held in a juvenile-justice residential placement. Additionally, 9,300 children are held in adult jails and prisons. More than 1.6 million children are involved in the juvenile justice system each year. Most remain in their parents' or guardians' custody. For those who become wards of the state, about one-third enter the child welfare system, while the other two-thirds enter the juvenile detention system.

According to the New York State Office of Children and Family Services (2011), 44 percent of juveniles released from residential care in 2008 were rearrested for a felony within two years. Glaze and Maruschak (2010, 1) noted that "1,706,600 minor children, accounting for 2.3 percent of the resident population under 18 [have a parent in prison]." Having a parent in prison places children at risk of continuing the pattern.

Other Risk Categories

Children who experience hunger, abuse, or exploitation, or who have a parent in prison are clearly at risk, and there are millions of such children. Yet the characteristics that place a child in the at-risk category also include a long list that incorporates a significant portion of the nation's school-age children. Included on that list are circumstances such as being: from a single-parent family, transient, overage/undercredited, truant, working instead of going to school, a parent, from a low socioeconomic status background, an English-language learner, and a foster child.

Wald and Martinez (2003) estimated that at any given time, approximately 1 million youth aged 14 to 17 fall into one of four major at-risk categories: 500,000 dropouts; 100,000 incarcerated; 338,000 foster children; and 175,000 unwed mothers. Because Wald and Martinez's numbers are based on cross-sectional data, they do not reflect the total number of young people who will fall into one of those categories. They estimated that 20 percent of 14- to 17-year-olds, more than 3 million youth in all, will fit into one of those four categories before they turn 18.

In recent years, a new type of at-risk youth has arisen: unaccompanied alien children. According to the U.S. Customs and Border Protection Administration of the Department of Homeland Security, 39,000 unaccompanied minors crossed the U.S.–Mexico border in fiscal year 2013. That number jumped in fiscal year 2014 to 69,000 unaccompanied children and youth entering the United States. Where the number of unaccompanied children entering the United States from Mexico has held steady—around 16,000—since 2009, the number of children from El Salvador, Guatemala, and Honduras has skyrocketed, from 1,200, 1,100, and 1,000 to 16,000, 17,000, and 18,000, respectively (U.S. Customs and Border Protection 2014).

Besides the 50 million children who attend America's public schools, another 6 million children attend our country's private and parochial schools. While private schools face issues with at-risk students, the overwhelming percentage of children who are hungry or migrant, who have been abused, exploited, are homeless, or have a parent in prison, attend public schools. The public schools do not cause their hunger or abuse or exploitation; they do not place children at risk. At the same time, the schools, charged with providing education, the lifeline to a better life, the best chance to break the cycle of poverty or abuse and improve the future, are often unsuccessful with the at-risk population.

AT-RISK IN SCHOOL

While there have been students at risk throughout the history of public education, and undoubtedly before, research on such students gained momentum in the mid-1960s following the initiation of Title 1, and it further accelerated after the coining of the term "at risk" by the National Commission of Excellence in Education's landmark publication, *A Nation at Risk*. Although there is no specific or universal definition of what it means to be an at-risk student, several researchers have come up with practical descriptions. Sagor and Cox (2004, 1) offered this definition of a student at risk: "any child who is unlikely to graduate, on schedule, with both the skills and self-esteem necessary to exercise meaningful options in the areas of work, leisure, culture, civic affairs, and inter/intrapersonal relationships." Slavin and Madden (2004) noted that at-risk children usually have one or more of the following characteristics: retention in grade level, poor attendance, behavioral problems, low socioeconomic status or poverty, low achievement, substance abuse, or teenage pregnancy.

The majority of children matriculate through their school years with success, but a significant number do not. At-risk students too often live in academic failure and pour like water through the fingers of schools' best efforts. The documentation of their exits from schools, and the circumstances that frame these, are clear:

- Every 26 seconds of every day, a student drops out of school; some 1.3 million students drop out of school each year (America's Promise 2011).
- In 2012, 1,359 high schools were considered dropout factories, where the senior class lost at least 40 percent of the students who started as freshmen (Balfanz, Bridgeland, Hornig et al. 2014).
- Given the normal distribution of intelligence, there are perhaps 8 million school children with low average intelligence (two standard deviations below the mean). These children have no diagnosable disability with which to qualify for special education. The nation's drive to raise standards and increase requirements for matriculation and graduation is taking a serious toll on this slice of young Americans.
- The study by Fableo, Thompson, Plotkin, and colleagues (2011) found that 31 percent of Texas students were suspended off campus or were expelled at least once during their years in middle and high school. When also considering less-serious infractions punished by in-school suspensions, the rate climbed to nearly 60 percent, with one in seven students facing such disciplinary measures at least 11 times. The study linked these disciplinary actions to lower rates of graduation and higher rates of later criminal activity and found that minority students were more likely than whites to face more severe punishments.
- Losen and Skiba (2010) report that suspension from school is far more prevalent today than it was in the 1970s. Driven by the wide adoption of zero-tolerance policies, suspension rates have more than doubled for nonwhite students, with blacks now three times more likely to be suspended than whites.

Public schools remain the best hope for most at-risk students, but there are processes, attitudes, and policies that place millions of at-risk children further at risk and at a great fiscal cost. Putting a total cost to America for the situations and events that place children at risk is a giant undertaking. Nonetheless, some data points are clear.

According to Levin and Rouse (2012), programs that successfully move an at-risk student through high-school graduation confer a net benefit to taxpayers of some $127,000 over a graduate's lifetime. Cutting the number of dropouts in half will save the nation nearly $90 billion a year, or around $1 trillion over 11 years. The Center for Labor Market Studies (2009) reports that there are more than 6 million dropouts between the ages of 16 and 24. The economic impact on those that left school early is devastating. Dropouts make $9,000 less a year than high-school graduates and $35,000 less than those with a college degree—$1.6 million less over a lifetime.

If money could solve this problem, it would have been solved decades ago. America gives generously and spends tax dollars liberally to finance the treatment of symptoms and the eradication of causes, but situations that place children at risk rage on. Millions of children make up the at-risk population. These are not only children who remain strangers to the basic comforts of middle-class America—food, clothing, shelter, freedom from fear, from want, from exploitation—but these are also children at risk of failing to receive a basic education. These are America's at-risk students.

AT-RISK AND ALTERNATIVE EDUCATION

Not all students who are at risk attend alternative-education programs, but it is a safe assumption that all students who attend alternative programs are at risk. Alternative-education programs are frequently found in American public-school districts, but they have not been widely studied. Information that is especially lacking includes how these programs are organized and administered, the certifications of staff members who teach and work in the schools, the curriculum, the manner in which the students are placed in the alternative programs and how they exit them, the programs' efficacy with students, their quality, and the impact they have on mainstream education.

Carver and Lewis (2010, 1) state:

> Alternative schools and programs are designed to address the needs of students that typically cannot be met in regular schools. The students who attend alternative schools and programs are typically at risk of education failure (as indicated by poor grades, truancy, disruptive behavior, pregnancy, or similar factors associated with temporary or permanent withdrawal from school). Further, the NCES notes that alternative schools are usually housed in separate facilities, while alternative programs are usually housed in the regular school.

In September 2002 and again in March 2010, the National Center for Education Statistics (NCES) published *Alternative Schools and Programs for Public School Students At Risk of Education Failure*. The initial study by Kleiner, Porch, Farris, and Greene (2002) used data from the 2000–2001 academic year; the second report, by Carver and Lewis (2010), focused on the 2007–2008 school year. These reports were designed to "provide national estimates on the availability of alternative schools and programs for students at risk of educational failure in public school districts" (Carver and Lewis 2010, 1). These two studies represent the most comprehensive review of programs for at-risk students undertaken to date. Key findings from the 2007–2008 NCES report include:

- Sixty-four percent of school districts reported having at least one alternative school managed by the district or by another entity.
- There were 10,300 district-administered alternative-education schools and programs.
- There were 646,500 students enrolled in public-school districts attending alternative schools or programs for at-risk students.
- Approximately 60 percent of school districts in the Midwest, North, and West had alternative-education programs, while approximately 90 percent of the districts in the South had these programs.
- Of school districts with district-administered alternative-school programs, 96 percent had such programs for twelfth graders, while only 18 percent had alternative programs for fifth graders (Carver and Lewis 2010).

Alternative schools and programs are certainly a part of public-school districts. The types of schools and programs vary and may be mixed with other agencies and services, such as job-training opportunities, juvenile-justice programs, childcare, and night school. Despite their extensive presence and varied presentations, there is little research on their efficacy, and the number of students currently served is much smaller than the number of students likely to be at risk.

While alternative schools and programs have wide acceptance among school districts, they are not without their critics. The Southern Poverty Law Center (SPLC) favored the implementation of positive behavioral interventions and supports instead of many of the tactics currently used to address negative behavior. As the SPLC put it, "Many schools employ discipline methods that research tells us are counter-productive and lead to dropping out: suspensions, expulsions, placements in alternative schools and referral to [the] criminal justice system" (Southern Poverty Law Center 2008, 3).

Few students aspire to attend an alternative school. Such schools and programs have evolved in response to the realities of the era. The number of children at risk remains unacceptably high and persistent. Alternative schools are designed to meet the needs of at-risk students, keep them in school, move them toward graduation, return them to the mainstream, keep them out of jail, help them with parenting responsibilities, help them care for their own parents, and/or to teach them English—in short, to help them overcome the very factors that make them at risk. Alternative education for at-risk students is a large undertaking, one worth doing as effectively as possible. The lives of millions of students hang in the balance.

CLEAR NEED BUT NO CLEAR PATH

Approximately 1.5 percent of 7.5 million students with IEPs attend a private school via a PPP. That's roughly 112,000 students involved in special-education PPPs. It's hardly possible to estimate the percent of at-risk students engaged in PPPs because neither the numerator nor the denominator of the equation is known. The only hard number regarding students enrolled in alternative-education programs comes from the above-cited NCES study: some 646,500 students. If these were the only students at risk in the country, what a wonderful world it would be.

The various categories of at-risk factors such as homelessness, hunger, or having a parent in prison are by no means mutually exclusive, but every school administrator knows that a significant portion of the district's students, sometimes as many as 100 percent, are at risk. Regardless of the categories examined or the filters used, there are millions of at-risk students in America. And the education of at-risk students is a core business for public education, or so it would seem.

The AASA's Dan Domenech recognizes the conundrum facing America's schools. He noted, "With higher standards come higher failure rates. This is obviously a huge problem. If we keep doing business as usual we can easily predict higher failure rates, lower college attendance rates, and higher dropout rates. We can't raise standards and leave the system alone. There is a role for public–private partnerships for at-risk students. The private sector and corporations' support can be huge" (personal communication, September 9, 2014).

Unlike special education where IDEA clearly sets the rules, no such corresponding regulations exist to address the millions of students at risk, nor are there corresponding national advocacy groups to help shape at-risk education. School districts are forced to do the best they can with what they have. It is the students at risk who can have a negative impact on a school or district's key metrics such as attendance rates, incidents of violence, and test performance. Providing educational content and structures that keep at-risk students in school, off the streets, and moving forward with their lives accomplishes enormous good for the student, the school, and the community. PPPs can be helpful, but they can also be tough to establish.

The fact that educating at-risk students is a core function of public education presents a dilemma: because it is a core function, school districts are often resistant to asking for help. The mystery is this: if educating at-risk students is a core function, why do so many students drop out? Bill Milliken, the founder of CIS, said it plainly: "The majority of the kids who drop out are suffering from deficits that no curriculum can make up. . . . The deteriorating conditions that millions of families face makes it virtually impossible for the schools to fulfill this mission. They just don't have the resources or expertise to address the deficiencies" (Milliken 2007, 115).

CIS brings the community's resources inside the public school to address the nonacademic, health, and social-emotional deficits that prevent students from succeeding. These community-based student-support services supplement the structure and curriculum provided within the school. "CIS is there to free the teachers up to teach," Milliken said (personal communication, October 21, 2014).

In his book, *The Last Dropout*, Milliken offers point after point that strike at the heart of the dropout crisis:

- "We don't have a youth problem in America—we have an adult problem" (p. 18).
- "We expect teachers and school administrators to be mother, father, sister, brother, counselor, social worker, good cop, bad cop—and also be great teachers" (p. 19).
- "Educators no longer have to go it alone, overextended and ill-equipped for the demands being placed on them" (p. 133).
- "We must scratch where people are itching" (p. 131).

Milliken also makes a point, especially coming from his nonprofit organization, that addresses the role of investment in solving an education dilemma:

> The word *charity* is really a synonym for *giving*, for providing resources. In the business world, no one calls it charity, of course, but every time a CEO approves a budget item for a particular project, he or she is making a decision to *give*, to *invest*, to allocate resources in the expectation of accomplishing an objective. Similarly, a local government agency that approves a grant to fund, say, a reading initiative in the public school system, is approving a particular type of gift.
>
> But if the system needs to change, all of the giving and investing won't make enough of a difference. When people talk about the uselessness of "throwing money at a problem," this is what they mean. Always remember, though, that once the necessary transformation has been effected, the resources must continue. Now we're no longer "throwing money," we're using it to fund a truly effective plan. (Milliken 2007, 130)

Milliken, with his 50 years in the trenches, provides a rationale for PPPs, nonprofit and for-profit: invest in what works; find the solution and keep funding it. And what is it that programs like CIS and ESA's Ombudsman bring to public schools that they can't do themselves or can't do as well as a private partner? It boils down to elements like focus, expertise, organizational structure, and mission. These programs are good at what they do and they are widely needed. Milliken said, "When any superintendent tells me that his district doesn't need help with at-risk kids, I send him an AA [Alcoholics Anonymous] book because he's in denial" (personal communication, October 21, 2014).

Ralph Thompson was an assistant superintendent for the Metropolitan Nashville Public Schools. In his role he oversaw the management of the PPP with Ombudsman Educational Services. When Thompson retired from his leadership position with the 80,000-student district, he joined ESA, the parent company of Ombudsman. Thompson remembers the process of bringing Ombudsman into the Metro Nashville schools. "It was no secret, Nashville was not unique. We had issues like poverty and discipline problems particularly related to at-risk children of color.

"Prior to Ombudsman, we talked about what we could do to address this issue. A lower pupil-teacher ratio was a key, along with an individualized academic program. Metro could provide wrap-around services. Nashville also had a high suspension rate and we know we can't teach students if they're not in school."

Thompson shared, "A couple of days after hearing the Ombudsman presentation, I was asked to design a similar program that we could do ourselves. It quickly became clear that Metro could not create a comparable program. Creating the program, getting the needed decision makers engaged, was too time-consuming. Plus, we'd have to hire additional teaching staff, find the needed facilities, and engage HR. It would consume too many resources and the district didn't have that kind of time. When you put it down on paper, you realized it couldn't be done.

"Ombudsman came in and did it all: the facilities, the technology, the staffing, and the academic programming. And I am glad to say, Ombudsman dropped the suspension rate in the district 17 percent in the first year," Thompson noted (personal communication, October 21, 2014).

Steve Joel, the superintendent in Lincoln, Nebraska, said, "We had Ombudsman when I was superintendent at Grand Island. We had no way in Grand Island to create the expertise Ombudsman has. Ombudsman has a great niche, a turnkey solution for at-risk students for a district without a good alternative education program. One of the benefits of an association with Ombudsman is that it is a fixed dollar amount. The additional personnel they bring in doesn't show up on the district's roll" (personal communication, October 13, 2014).

Before Howard Hinesley took the superintendency at the 4,000-student Cartersville Public School District in Georgia, he spent 1990 to 2004 in Florida as superintendent of the 100,000-student Pinellas County Schools. Hinesley's 46 years in public education, 25 as a superintendent, make him one of the country's most experienced active district leaders. He reflected, "We were looking for an alternative-education program, and after research Ombudsman surfaced quickly. We toured the Ombudsman program in another district, and I engaged the school board, and I got them on board. In the end we wound up with a really good partnership.

"The teachers work to identify kids who really need the program. We don't use it as a dumping ground. We put a screening process in place and hold seats available as needed. Ombudsman gives individual attention with the goal of returning the students to the high school; if that does not happen, the students can also complete high school through Ombudsman. The impact on the mainstream has been tremendous. The teachers say Ombudsman has been a blessing" (personal communication, October 24, 2014).

With some 127 alternative programs in 17 states, Ombudsman is the nation's largest private alternative-education partner for school districts. Even so, the number of at-risk students it reaches is hardly a blip on the at-risk screen. Despite being successful with 80 percent of the students it enrolls by either returning them to the district with improved skills and increased credits earned or seeing them through graduation, Ombudsman only enrolled some 12,000 in the 2013–2014 school year. And the political challenges that come with doing business with public schools are enough to frustrate the most seasoned government relations advisor. Absurdities are the rule, not the exception.

It is the regime-change phenomenon that leaves Ombudsman vulnerable, a business problem that haunts all companies engaged in PPPs. As related in chapter 2, the founder of Netflix noted that it is difficult to do business with public school districts due to the lack of continuity at the top. Superintendent Hinesley knows that PPPs can be vulnerable to regime changes and that he won't be a superintendent forever. As such, he writes contracts with partners that will live beyond his resignation. He noted, "Sometimes superintendents will change stuff just to change it. Part of leadership is if something is working, leave it alone" (personal communication, October 24, 2014).

Despite the wisdom of Hastings and Hinesley, successful PPPs are often out the door with a new superintendent. Indeed, a change of superintendents is a threat for PPPs. What's the new superintendent expected to do? In nearly all cases, he or she is expected to bring in new ideas, to do things differently. The new superintendent can't fire the administrative team, can't dismiss staff, can't irritate the school board (at least not immediately). PPPs! Aha, there's a change that can be made without expending political capital.

The risks inherent in creating a PPP for at-risk students are substantial for the private company. There is a long sales cycle: six to 12 months is typical and multiple years is not unusual. Even with the support of the superintendent, the school board must approve the contract. Most alternative-education programs are off-site in properly sized and zoned facilities that must be secured and built out. Staff must be hired and trained, equipment and technology installed.

Hundreds of thousands to millions of dollars are invested by the private partner before any revenue, much less profit, is realized in the hope that the PPP will be successful. All the time, the private entity has little control of the contract and serves at the will of a public district, which cannot encumber money beyond the current fiscal year and is led by a superintendent's office that changes occupants like a barber's chair.

In fact, a recent survey conducted by the Council of Great City Schools showed that the average tenure of superintendents lost ground. Of its 66 members, 53 responded to the survey. These superintendents lead some of the nation's largest districts. According to the survey, the average time in the position slipped from 3.64 years in 2010 to 3.18 years in 2014. Michael Casserly, the council executive director, noted, "This continued churn makes it harder for urban school systems to maintain and accelerate the positive academic momentum that they have created over the last several years" (Will 2014).

Despite the challenges, PPPs for students at risk continue. Of the 127 Ombudsman programs across the country, most enroll around 100 students and are off campus in strip malls or business office locations with easy access to public transportation. But in recent years, school districts have asked Ombudsman to take on larger numbers of more complex students. Here are some examples:

- Sioux Falls, South Dakota, is a United Nations High Commissioner for Refugees resettlement city. In the past decade, thousands of refugees from Laos, Bhutan, Nepal, Guatemala, Sudan, Somalia, Rwanda, and other countries have been resettled in this city of 150,000. When older teens with limited to no English-language skills arrive, the Sioux Falls Public School District provides the students with a choice to enter one of the mainstream high schools or attend the Presidents' Academy, operated by Ombudsman. The Presidents' Academy features low pupil-teacher ratios, the chance of accelerated credit production, and a quiet, self-contained environment. The Presidents' Academy is located within the district's technical and career high school, which allows these new Americans access to the development of job skills. In addition, Ombudsman operates Joe Foss High School, the long-standing alternative high school within the district. Total enrollment in both programs is approximately 400 students.
- The Chicago Public Schools (CPS) established PPPs during the 2013–2014 academic year with a variety of for-profit and nonprofit organizations to address the desire to retrieve thousands of students who have dropped out. Ombudsman is contracted to serve 1,600 students in three schools that Ombudsman built in locations suitable to CPS. No surplus CPS properties were made available via the PPP arrangement.
- In the Caddo Parish School District in Louisiana, Ombudsman operates seven alternative-education programs for students assigned by the district. Ombudsman was brought in by a superintendent who was seeking better outcomes than the district was producing in its own alternative programs. Approximately 400 students attend Ombudsman programs in Caddo Parish.
- The Savannah Chatham County School District in Georgia needed an appropriate setting for students interacting with the juvenile court system. Ombudsman established four learning centers and works with the schools and the court system in providing

an alternative-learning opportunity for approximately 350 students.

- In the Philadelphia School District, Ombudsman developed programs to support the district's Alternative Education for Disrupted Youth Program. Three Ombudsman centers serve a total of 175 students in the Philadelphia area. Ombudsman is part of a portfolio of private partners for the Philadelphia public schools, each with a different expertise.

Camelot Education, based in Austin, Texas, provides partnership schools for at-risk students. Camelot offers Accelerated Education Schools in three states and Transitional Programs in five. Below are examples of each:

- Camelot's two Excel Academies in Philadelphia focus on overage, undercredentialed at-risk high-school students termed "near dropout" students. Students who enroll at Excel must be at least 16 years of age and have two or fewer accumulated credits toward graduation. Excel offers the full complement of courses needed for students to acquire the 23.5 credits the district requires for graduation. Once enrolled, students receive an individualized and accelerated curriculum designed to keep them engaged in school. Camelot provides them with a curriculum framework that enables them to graduate in 2.5 years or less. The Excel class of 2011 boasted 380 graduates.
- Camelot's transitional school in Camden, New Jersey, is tailored to the specific needs and objectives of the district, offering remedial discipline as well as specialized dropout-prevention programs. It has a maximum enrollment of 150 students ranging in age from 11 to 17. Students are referred to the program by the Camden school district for violations of its code of conduct.

Public education is tasked with an ever-growing list of duties, possibly an absurd amount of responsibilities. Schooling is perhaps the last open-ended entitlement in the nation. With the collapse of a sense of community, with the changes in the nature of family, with increasing numbers of new Americans arriving daily, at-risk students are no longer the exception; they are becoming the rule.

Reaching at-risk students is a core function of public schooling. But given the wildly diverse nature of at-risk students, a single core program is wildly inadequate. The national numbers speak for themselves. It is entirely unrealistic to expect public schools to meet the needs of such a broad band of students. One size never fits all and even chocolate, vanilla, and strawberry options can't do the job today. Niche programs offered in PPPs like Ombudsman, CIS, Camelot, and others leverage resources and offer hope.

Despite the exponentially expanded functions of public education, schools are absurdly measured by a single function, one metric of success: academic performance. Qualitative indicators that measure the impact schools have on the lives of children are heaped in the dust bin. It's a preposterous dynamic, but one that is likely to continue and one that is likely to operate even less effectively tomorrow than it does today.

At-risk factors affect millions of America's schoolchildren. Without laws equivalent to IDEA, without advocacy organizations as effective as Autism Speaks, the leaders of public education have only their wits and determination to address the complex issue of reducing the dropout rate, increasing the graduation rate, and moving millions of at-risk students to a better future. PPPs are one of the simplest, most economically efficient, and most academically effective measures schools have at their fingertips.

REFERENCES

America's Promise. 2011. "26 Seconds" Campaign to Engage Youth at Risk of Dropping Out. Retrieved from http://www.americaspromise.org/News-and-Events/News-and-Features/2011-News/March/State-Farm-26-Seconds-launch.aspx.

Annie E. Casey Foundation. n.d. *No Place for Kids: The Case for Reducing Juvenile Incarceration*. (Issue Brief). Retrieved from http://www.aecf.org/~/media/Pubs/Topics/Juvenile percent20Justice/Detention percent20Reform/NoPlaceforKidsIssueBrief/JJ_DeepEnd_IssueBrief.pdf.

Balfanz, R., Bridgeland, J., Hornig Fox, J., DePaoli, J. L., Ingram, E. S., and Maushard, M. 2014. Building a GradNation: Progress and Challenge in Ending the High School Dropout Epidemic. Retrieved from http://gradnation.org/sites/default/files/17548_BGN_Report_FinalFULL_5.2.14.pdf.

Califano, J. A., Jr. 2010. Requiring Parents to Send Children to Gang- and Drug-Infested Schools Is State-Sanctioned Child Abuse. *Huffington Post*, August 30. Retrieved from http://www.casacolumbia.org/newsroom/op-eds/requiring-parents-send-children-gang-and-drug-infected-schools-state-sanctioned.

Cartledge, G., and Dukes, C. 2009. Disproportionality of African American Children in Special Education: Definition and Dimensions. In *The Sage Handbook of African American Education*, 383–98, ed. L. C. Tilman. Thousand Oaks, CA: Sage Publications.

Carver, P. R., and Lewis, L. 2010. *Alternative Schools and Programs: Public School Students at Risk of Education Failure: 2007–08* (NCES 2010-026). U.S. Department of Education, National Center for Education Statistics. Washington, DC: Government Printing Office.

Centers for Disease Control and Prevention. 2013. Adverse Childhood Experiences (ACE) Study. Retrieved from http://www.cdc.gov/ace/prevalence.htm.

Center for Labor Market Studies. 2009. *Left Behind in America: The Nation's Dropout Crisis*. Northeastern University Center of Labor Market Studies Publications. Paper 21. Retrieved from http://iris.lib.neu.edu/cgi/viewcontent.cgi?article=1020&context=clms_pub.

Child Molestation and Prevention Institute. 2014. Child Molestation Prevention Plan. Retrieved from http://www.childmolestationprevention.org/pages/prevention_plan.html.

Children's Defense Fund. 2012. Juvenile Justice. Retrieved from http://www.childrensdefense.org/policy-priorities/juvenile-justice/.

Coleman-Jensen, A., Nord, M., and Singh, A. 2013. *Household Food Security in the United States in 2012*. Economic Research Report 155, Economic Research Service/U.S. Department of Agriculture, September 2013.

Estes, R. J., and Weiner, N. A. 2002. *The Commercial Sexual Exploitation of Children in the U.S., Canada and Mexico*. Philadelphia: University of Pennsylvania. Retrieved from https://maggiemcneill.files.wordpress.com/2011/04/estes-weiner-2001.pdf.

Fabelo, T., Thompson, M. D., Plotkin, M., Carmichael, D., Marchbanks, M. P., and Booth, E. A. 2011. *Breaking Schools' Rules: A Statewide Study of How School Discipline Relates to Students' Success and Juvenile Justice Involvement*. New York: Council of State Government Justice Center.

Feeding America. 2014. The Impact of Hunger. Retrieved from http://feedingamerica.org/hunger-in-america/impact-of-hunger.aspx.

Glaze, L. E., and Maruschak, L. M. 2010. *Parents in Prison and Their Minor Children*. Washington, DC: U.S. Department of Justice, Bureau of Justice Statistics. Retrieved from http://www.bjs.gov/content/pub/pdf/pptmc.pdf.

Human Rights Watch. 2000. Adolescent Farm Workers in the United States: Endangerment and Exploitation. In *Fingers to the Bone: United States Failure to Protect Child Farmworkers*. New York: Human Rights Watch. Retrieved from http://www.hrw.org/reports/2000/frmwrkr/frmwrk006-02.htm -P269_31143.

Kleiner, B., Porch, R., Farris, E., and Greene, B. 2002. *Public Alternative Schools and Programs for Students at Risk of Educational Failure: 2000–01*. (NCES 2002-004). U.S. Department of Education, National Center for Education Statistics. Washington, DC: Government Printing Office.

Levin, H. M., and Rouse, C. E. 2012. "The True Cost of High School Dropouts." *New York Times,* January 26, A31. Retrieved from http://www.nytimes.com/2012/01/26/opinion/the-true-cost-of-high-school-dropouts.html?_r=0.

Losen, D. J., and Skiba, R. J. 2010. *Suspended Education: Urban Middle Schools in Crisis*. Montgomery, AL: Southern Poverty Law Center. Retrieved from http://www.splcenter.org/sites/default/files/downloads/publication/Suspended_Education.pdf.

Milliken, B. 2007. *The Last Dropout: Stop the Epidemic*. Carlsbad, CA: Hay House.

National Center on Family Homelessness. 2010. *America's Youngest Outcasts 2010: State Report Card on Child Homelessness*. Retrieved from http://www.homelesschildrenamerica.org/.

National Coalition for the Homeless. 2009. *How Many People Experience Homelessness?* Retrieved from http://www.nationalhomeless.org/factsheets/How_Many.pdf.

National Scientific Council on the Developing Child. 2005/2014. Excessive Stress Disrupts the Architecture of the Developing Brain: Working Paper 3. Updated edition. Retrieved from www.developingchild.harvard.edu.

New York State Office of Child and Family Services. 2011. *OFCS Fact Sheet: Recidivism among Juvenile Delinquents and Offenders Released from Residential Care in 2008*. Retrieved   from   http://ocfs.ny.gov/main/detention_reform/Recidivism   percent20fact percent20sheet.pdf.

Sagor, R., and Cox, J. 2004. *At-Risk Students: Reaching Them and Teaching Them*. Larchmont, NY: Eye on Education.

Slavin, R., and Madden, N. 2004. *Students At-Risk of School Failure: The Problem of Its Dimensions*. Johns Hopkins University Center for Research on Elementary and Middle Schools: Boston: Allyn and Bacon.

Southern Poverty Law Center. 2008, July. *Effective Discipline for Student Success: Reducing Student and Teacher Dropout Rates in Alabama*. Retrieved from http://www.splcenter. org/sites/default/files/downloads/Effective_Discipline_ALA.pdf.

United States Census Bureau. 2012. Poverty Highlights. Retrieved from http://www.census. gov/hhes/www/poverty/about/overview/index.html.

United States Customs and Border Protection. 2014. Southwest Boarder Unaccompanied Alien Children. Retrieved from http://www.cbp.gov/newsroom/stats/southwest-border-unaccompanied-children.

United States Department of Education, National Center for Educational Statistics. 2012. Fast Facts. Retrieved from http://nces.ed.gov/fastfacts/display.asp?id=65.

United States Department of Health and Human Services, Administration for Children and Families. 2013, December. Fewer Child Abuse and Neglect Victims for Sixth Consecutive Year. Retrieved from http://www.acf.hhs.gov/press/fewer-child-abuse-and-neglect-victims-for-sixth-consecutive-year.

Wald, M., and Martinez, T. 2003. *Connected by 25: Improving the Life Chances of the Country's Most Vulnerable 14–24-Year-Olds*. William and Flora Hewlett Foundation Working Paper.

Will, M. 2014, November 6. Average Urban School Superintendent Tenure Decreases, Survey Shows [Education Week's Blogs]. Retrieved from http://blogs.edweek.org/edweek/ District_Dossier/2014/11/urban_school_superintendent_te.html.

7

A TRAIL TO THE FUTURE

Where all the women are strong, the men are good looking, and all the children are above average. —Garrison Keillor

If every child who showed up at school was well fed, well rested, and eager to learn, the performance of public schooling would measurably increase and cost would measurably decrease. If every child with autism received appropriate therapy and made maximum progress, the lifetime cost of care for those children who still could not enter the mainstream would drop substantially. But those are big ifs. Millions of hungry, tired, homeless, and abused children show up at the schoolhouse gate, as do almost a half million children with autism. The parents of untreated or undertreated children with autism watch years go by and the chance for minimizing the disease with them.

Public education with its common purpose and progressive foundation finds itself burdened beyond belief, the proverbial camel waiting for one more straw. Consider the roles that public schools play beyond academics:

- Respite provider for working parents.
- Safe harbor for neglected children.
- Sports entertainment venue for the local community.
- Farm system for college athletics.
- Instiller of social values.
- College prep for many students not interested in or suited for college.

- Educator almost devoid of teaching meaningful trade skills.
- Warrior against drug and alcohol abuse.
- Primary nutrition center.
- Character educator.
- Desegregator of society.
- Gender equalizer.
- Smoking discourager.
- Abstinence educator.
- Pregnancy preventer.
- STD preventer.
- Child-abuse monitor.
- After-school care provider.
- Gang-involvement discourager.
- Driver educator.
- Bullying preventer.
- Internet-safety educator.
- Obesity monitor.
- Social-media etiquette trainer.
- Steroid-abuse preventer.
- Intruder lockdown trainer.
- Financial-literacy developer.

The list continues with scores of additional items that have been placed under the care of public education. All of them are important. All are worthy of time and attention.

But squeezed among all these responsibilities is the passing of knowledge and the development of academic and intellectual skills as measured by test scores, the only function of schools that gets measured and that matters in the eyes of those who have created the standards of today. The performance of a school in all the areas noted above may mean a great deal to the students and their families, but at the end of the day, proficiency in those responsibilities can't keep a school off the F list.

Schools reflect the societies they serve. America is a wonderful and noble place, but it is imperfect and many of its imperfections and dys-functions are mirrored in its schools. The obsession with test scores that our nation has developed is unfortunate. This obsession is manifested far more by its political leaders and a business community fixated on international competition and workers to fit into a changing economy than the average citizen who certainly wants children to learn but also sees schools as crucial to providing the noncore functions noted above.

The dirty little secret in raising the bar and increasing standards is that it won't change average intelligence in America. By definition, 50 percent of America's children will remain below average regardless of how high standards are increased. Rather, raising the bar will leave millions of students even further disenfranchised. The back doors of public schools will grow wider as those left behind exit the public-school system. There is no Lake Wobegone effect to be had; all children will not be above average.

Already schools reflect these new realities. Consider the frequency and significance of cheating scandals that have rocked school districts and entire states. Consider the complex bureaucracies in states like Michigan that inhibit the retrieval of dropouts into recovery programs. Consider the fact that California does not consider a student a dropout unless or until he or she signs the appropriate paperwork.

There is a perfect storm brewing. The midterm elections of 2014 saw a repudiation of liberal ideas and significant gains made by school-choice and charter advocates. School-choice policies are crucial matters for key Republicans with higher office aspirations such as Senators Rand Paul and Marco Rubio. A combination of an aging population, technological capacities, and fiscal woes is pushing against the concept of public education as we have known it. As school leaders respond to pressures laying more responsibilities on the system and simultaneously fostering more options for competition, aggressive public-education ad-ministrators will bring to bear every efficient and effective solution they can harness, including PPPs.

There is far more right than wrong with American public education. Tearing down the existing system isn't the answer. But schools must read the signs of the times and adjust and adapt. The monolith of public education is comprised of 50 state systems further subdivided into 14,000 districts made up of 99,000 schools. They have never moved as a unit or in lock step. Witness the extreme variation of the implementa-tion of IDEA as described in chapter 4.

The market-based solutions championed by choice advocates push against the disappointments of public schools and work to empower parents to select the education option they deem best for their children.

There is absolutely no reason public schools cannot compete, hold, and gain ground in this battle for market share. Again, a chief ally in this battle can and should be PPPs.

In the arena of special education, historical, regulatory, geographic, and cultural factors have been paramount in determining the use of PPPs to serve children with exceptionalities. For those states where special-education PPPs are common, there is no reason to see an erosion of those well-defined processes. In states with large areas and sparse populations, the realities of a needed critical mass make the utilization of PPPs difficult. States with significant populations, where PPPs in special education are infrequent, should not wait for advocacy groups and attorneys to force the issue; states should take the lead.

Furthermore, public schools should compete with one another to have the very best, most cutting-edge special-education programs. How lucky a school district will be to have people move into their community to participate in a model program. That represents growth for the community, an asset for employers wanting to attract top-flight employees, and progress for chambers of commerce wanting to bring new industry to the community. Who loses if all school districts create outstanding special-education programs? No one.

Market-based efforts have been embraced by public education from coast to coast. Open enrollment, postsecondary enrollment options, magnet schools, and district charters are all efforts to expand choice for families and to compete with other public and private schools. Why not add excellent special-education programs to that list?

Whether autism will be divorced from IDEA is a long-term question. In the meantime, public education can stand with advocacy groups and parents in their battle to get health insurance to cover autism. Selfishly, public education has nothing to lose and so much to gain by having fewer children with more serious conditions needing special-education services.

It is the arena of at-risk education where public education can become creative and market-savvy. Alternative education is at the regulatory edge of schooling. As such, creativity is the order of the day. Unfortunately, many district-sponsored alternative-education programs are staffed like James Buchanan High in the 1970s television comedy *Welcome Back Kotter*. The Sweathogs were housed on the top floor of the un-air-conditioned school and Vice Principal Michael Woodman repeatedly advised Gabe Kotter not to try to teach his students, just attempt to contain them.

Currently there are no certifications for alternative-education teachers or administrators and few guidelines for school organization. That presents an opportunity for effective creativity, to develop learning environments where at-risk students can grow and thrive using blended learning, low pupil-to-teacher ratios, shorter days, and mastery learning. These out-of-the-box solutions are what PPPs in alternative education provide.

Public education does not want to maintain the status quo. Adopting a bunker mentality, raising the drawbridge and trying to wait out the siege, is not a winning strategy. Public schools can't do it alone, and embracing PPPs is not an admission of failure. It's embracing a tool to expand the district's portfolio of offerings. It's a performance contract to be managed.

Public education has the opportunity to flip the narrative and shift the view of public schooling from a tax burden to a revenue generator. Great public schools are great for the community. They foster higher tax revenue. They foster happier parents and happier employees. They foster safer communities. They foster better community engagement. They bring the public back to public education.

THE VALUE OF SPECIALISTS

Here are two examples from other industries of why schools can benefit from the expertise of groups that focus on nothing but alternative or special education. In building a home, a general contractor brings together the many crafts needed. None of those craftspeople can complete the entire house. HVAC people don't do plumbing and plumbers don't do electrical work. If a general contractor says he has painters who could build the entire house, a new general contractor is needed.

Similarly, if you have had a chronic problem with your knee and you set an appointment with your family practitioner for a referral to an orthopedist, you would probably be put off if your family practitioner offered to operate on your knee and was insulted when you said you wanted to see a specialist—a doctor who does knees and only knees.

So it can be with public schools. The argument that at-risk education is a core function does not hold in light of the dropout rate. The argument that public education has to be everything to everybody is as antiquated as public phone booths. Public education is the new generalist, the primary care physician effectively treating the vast percentage of patients seen every day, but also willing to refer to a specialist as needed.

Our public schools can think of themselves as a general contractor bringing partners into the district to complement its strengths and shore up its weaknesses. Specialists like CIS help keep students in school, and Ombudsman effectively educates at-risk students and enhances credit recovery. Specialists like ACES in Phoenix or Spectrum in California provide the appropriate setting for students according to the IEP team's directive.

School districts are organizations like businesses, churches, nonprofits, and universities. As such, there is much to be learned from the experiences of other groups in general and specifically about the importance of stability and planned transitions at the top and about using PPPs.

INSIGHTS FROM ORGANIZATIONAL EXPERTS

Jim Collins and Seth Godin—two of the most notable organizational thinkers in the business world—have offered thoughts on how public education can improve. Each sees public schooling through a unique lens both organizationally and culturally. Below are slices of their insights.

In 2003, Jim Collins' *Good to Great: Why Some Companies Make the Leap . . . And Others Don't* was at peak impact. In applying his research to public education, Collins was deeply respectful of the difficulty and complexity of leading a school district. In an interview with *The School Administrator*, Collins said, "I genuinely believe that being a superintendent of a large school district is more difficult than being CEO of a Fortune 500 corporation. . . . My perception after looking at lots of types of organizations and institutions is that the job of a school superintendent, particularly in a complicated community, is one of the hardest jobs in America" (Mast 2003).

In 2012, AASA Executive Director Dan Domenech interviewed Collins about what his research means for school leaders. In addressing the topic of mediocrity and the results of frequent superintendent changes, Collins said, "One of the things that we found in our research is that the signature of mediocrity is not an unwillingness to change—although, if indeed you do refuse to change, you will eventually fall behind. The real signature of mediocrity is chronic inconsistency. When you look inside the Beat the Odds Schools, we found they didn't keep changing every two years to try to find another program. They never believed there was a single-purpose program. Rather, they picked a good program and then marched with fanatic, consistent, relentless discipline to improve performance. Over time, through this consistency, they produced great results" (Domenech 2012, 41).

Seth Godin is not as kind to public schooling or its leaders. Godin wants outrage. In an August 2, 2013, discussion on WGBH's *Innovation Hub*, the former Yahoo! president said, "I just want, Alice's Restaurant-style, people to walk into the school board and say, 'What is school for,' and walk out," he said. "If we ask that question enough times, we'll get a shot at getting to teach the right thing—which is not obedience, not compliance, not adherence to normalcy, but the right thing is teaching kids to solve interesting problems and to lead" (Miller 2013).

In his manifesto *Stop Stealing Dreams*, Godin weaves together 132 short essays and blogs that lambaste the structure, purpose, and organization of Horace Mann's gift to the nation. Of those 132 blogs, two fit the current discussion:

#55. Make something differently

> The simple way to make something different is to go about it in a whole new way. In other words, doing what we're doing now and hoping we'll get something else as an outcome is nuts. Once we start to do schooling differently, we'll start to get something different. (Godin 2012, 42)

#111. Dumb as a choice

> Let's define dumb as being different from stupid.
> Dumb means you don't know what you're supposed to know. Stupid means you know it but make bad choices.

Access to information has radically changed in just 10 years. Kahn
Academy, Wikipedia, a hundred million blogs, and a billion web-
sites mean that if you're interested enough, you can find the
answer, wherever you are.

School, then, needs not to deliver information so much as to sell kids
on wanting to find it. (Godin 2012, 77)

Neither Collins nor Godin mention PPPs. They mention the challenges of leadership, the importance of persistence, the importance of
doing something differently to get different results, the ubiquity of
knowledge and the fact that all learning is self-learning. Each of those
points provide a foundation for school leaders to be open to opportunities presented through cooperation with specialists and staying a
course that educates the dumb and guides the stupid.

THE FUTURE OF PPPS

There is a realization and acceptance that the mission of public education has become so all-encompassing and the breadth of knowledge,
information, and technology so great that fulfilling the duties and cover-
ing the content has simply gone beyond what a school district could
efficiently and effectively deliver a generation ago. This is leading to a
sea change, a significant transformation, a new way of doing business.
Innovation, load sharing, and partnering are the order of the day for
successful schools. And at the state level there is a shift well under way
of moving away from being the deliverer and toward being the authorizer and regulator of schooling. A new normal is under development.

Bobbi Kurshan knows a thing or two about change. She is the executive director of academic innovation and a senior fellow at the Graduate
School of Education at the University of Pennsylvania. She has built
successful education-technology companies and has been recognized
for her contribution to education by groups ranging from the World
Innovation Summit for Education to the National Association of State
Boards of Education and UNESCO.

Kurshan said, "There is an absolute change in what people think
about partnerships. No longer is a public–private partnership a relationship between a seller and a buyer. It is now an innovative partnership.
We look at this as building a new ecosystem. More and more public

education is an equal partner, not a buyer of a service or a receiver of a donation. Now public schools are engaged as designers, researchers, and sometimes with teachers holding ownership in partnering companies. You can never have a partnership where one person holds more power than the other. You have to have a win-win for both sides. School districts in major urban areas are realizing that this is the only way to get their cities engaged."

As evidence of the importance of innovation and the need for true partnerships between entrepreneurs and school districts, the University of Pennsylvania is moving into its sixth Milken-Penn Graduate School of Education Educational Business Plan Competition. Kurshan provides executive-level leadership of the competition. "The Penn Business Plan Competition is a pipeline for innovation," she said. "It is judged by teachers, investors, and entrepreneurs. We engage potential users of a product from the start. Engaging stakeholders changes what people think about partnerships and moves us to an integrated synergistic ecosystem" (personal communication, November 13, 2014).

The sea change, the new ecosystem that Kurshan sees, is becoming evident in the departments of education in a handful of states. With various manifestations from special-education vouchers to allowing for-profit companies to hold charters, Florida, Arizona, Utah, and Indiana are shaping new public-education environments where the state is moving from provider to authorizer and where the emphasis is shifting from a focus on public education to a focus on the education of the public.

Joining these four states in creating education marketplaces is Louisiana, where John White has served as state superintendent for the past four years. He was appointed to the post after serving as a deputy chancellor in the New York City schools and as superintendent of the Louisiana Recovery School District. White is a proponent of changing the role of the state from provider to authorizer. He said, "States have been the regulator of a state service monopoly rather that an authorizer of service providers. States would be well advised to see themselves as the authorizer of educational services. Louisiana has created platforms exclusively to leverage private sector innovation. I believe that more states will move in this direction."

White sees technical and career education as a good example of why it is necessary to leverage the private sector. "Career education has made a big comeback. The plurality of offerings for those moving beyond high school into the work world is so great that it is crazy to think a high school can cover all of that. There is an obvious and evident need to find systemic ways to leverage the private sector. This is huge," he noted.

"There is a perception that a state chief is either a traditionalist or a choice person. But you can be agnostic and bring in the best by leveraging a wide array of capacities a school district rarely has. Louisiana authorizes a wide variety of capacities and we've learned so much. We have a common template for our authorizing process for things such as charters, nonpublic schools, and course-level services. We're only as good as our outcomes and we're not where we need to be, but we're moving in the right direction.

"When a state creates a process and accountability measures it can create a marketplace to solve problems. We don't have a choice. We can't solve child care, special education, and career and technical education without leveraging the private sector," White offered (personal communication, December 3, 2014).

FINAL THOUGHTS

American public education is responsible for creating its own future. Part of that future can be the greater utilization of PPPs. At a minimum, PPPs in special and at-risk education expand the capacity of a school district to meet the needs of its students. More often than not, however, such PPPs go far beyond providing minimal benefits to the partnering school district and provide fiscal, regulatory, and instructional benefits to the district, its students, and its community.

While PPPs won't take care of all the ills of public schooling, it is evident that the status quo is overwhelmed and endangered. PPPs can play a significant role in creating the future for public schooling by providing focused solutions and by involving the business community as partners in addressing complex and long-standing issues such as decreasing the dropout rate or more recent challenges like providing ABA for children with autism.

The comparison made in chapter 5 that medicine works toward the best option, a cure, or a ceiling for a child with autism whereas schools are allowed by law to merely provide a floor, or the minimum, is applicable to the future of public education. ABA works for children with autism. Appropriate alternative education can change the trajectory of an at-risk student's life. These are facts, not marketing claims. PPPs can help school districts better serve students with such needs. But to allow the treatment of ABA and the environment of alternative education to reach those who need them requires a core paradigm shift in public education away from compliance and the maintenance of the status quo and toward what works and toward a cure.

REFERENCES

Domenech, D. 2012, June. Jim Collins on mediocrity and the benefits of paranoia. *School Administrator* 6 (69): 40–43. Retrieved from http://www.aasa.org/content.aspx?id=23588.

Godin, S. 2012. *Stop Stealing Dreams*. Retrieved from http://www.sethgodin.com/sg/docs/stopstealingdreamsscreen.pdf.

Mast, C. 2003. Q & A with Jim Collins. *School Administrator* 11 (60). Retrieved from http://aasa.org/SchoolAdministratorArticle.aspx?id=8924.

Miller, Kara. 2013, August 2. "Seth Godin Indicts Education." WGBH. Retrieved from wgbhnews.org/post/seth-godin-indicts-education.

CONTRIBUTOR INDEX

ABOUT THE AUTHORS

Mark Claypool is president and CEO of Educational Services of America (ESA), which he founded in 1999. Prior to forming ESA, he held various positions in both state government and the private sector in mental health, juvenile corrections, and education. Today, ESA is the nation's leading provider of behavior therapy and alternative and special-education programs for children and young adults. ESA works with more than 13,500 clients and students each day across its three divisions: Early Autism Project, Ombudsman Educational Services, and Spectrum Center Schools and Programs. In addition, Claypool is president of the board of directors of Book'em, a Nashville nonprofit that seeks to inspire a love of books and reading in all children, and that collects and distributes books to children and teens who might not otherwise have books of their own. Through Book'em, he also serves as a volunteer reader at an urban elementary school. Claypool obtained a bachelor's degree in psychology and a master of arts in sociology from Middle Tennessee State University.

John M. McLaughlin, PhD, is an executive vice president and the director of research and analytics for Educational Services of America (ESA). He has been with the company since 1999. Prior to joining ESA, McLaughlin founded Benton Hall School in Nashville (1977), was a tenured professor of educational administration at St. Cloud State University in Minnesota (1988–1998), and wrote monthly on education reform in *The Education Industry Report* (1993–2000). He has spoken extensively on education to groups ranging from the American Association of School Administrators to the World Bank. His first book of fiction, *The Last Year of the Season* (North Star Press), was published in 2014. He holds degrees from Peabody College of Vanderbilt University, the University of Chicago, and the University of Minnesota.